American English File

Third Edition

Starter

MULTI-PACK **A**

Student Book | Workbook

Christina Latham-Koenig
Clive Oxenden
Jerry Lambert

Paul Seligson and Clive Oxenden
are the original co-authors of
English File 1 and *English File 2*

Contents

Course overview

American English File
Third Edition

Welcome to **American English File Third Edition**. This is how to use the Student Book, Online Practice, and the Workbook in and out of class.

Student Book

All the language and skills you need to improve your English, with Grammar, Vocabulary, Pronunciation, and skills work in every File.

Use your Student Book in class with your teacher.

Workbook

Grammar, Vocabulary, and Pronunciation practice for every lesson.

Use your Workbook for homework or for self-study to practice language and to check your progress.

Go to
americanenglishfileonline.com
and use the code on
your Access Card to
log into the Online
Practice.

ACTIVITIES   AUDIO   VIDEO   RESOURCES

ONLINE

LOOK AGAIN

- Review the language from every lesson.
- Watch the video and listen to all the class audio as many times as you like.

PRACTICE

- Improve your skills with extra Reading, Writing, Listening, and Speaking practice.
- Use the interactive video to practice Practical English.

CHECK YOUR PROGRESS

- Test yourself on the language from the File and get instant feedback.
  - Try a Challenge activity.

SOUND BANK

- Use the Sound Bank video to practice and improve your pronunciation of English sounds.

Online Practice

Look again at Student Book language you want to review or that you missed in class, do extra *Practice* activities, and *Check your progress* on what you learned so far.

Use the Online Practice to learn outside the classroom and get instant feedback on your progress.

americanenglishfileonline.com

Hi, I'm Helen.

Hello, I'm Tom. Nice to meet you.

G verb *be* (singular): *I* and *you* | **V** numbers 0–10, days of the week, saying goodbye | **P** /h/, /aɪ/, and /i/

1 LISTENING & SPEAKING

a 🔊 **1.2** Read and listen.

Helen	A cappuccino, please.
Barista 1	What's your name?
Helen	Helen.
Barista 1	Ellen?
Helen	No, Helen.
Barista 1	Helen. OK.

Barista 2	Are you Diana?
Helen	No, I'm not. I'm Helen.
Barista 2	Sorry.
	Helen? Your cappuccino.
Helen	Thanks.

Tom	Hello. Are you Helen?
Helen	Yes, I am. And you're Tom.
Tom	Yes! Nice to meet you.
Helen	Nice to meet you.
Tom	Just a minute.

Tom	Hi. A tea, please.
Barista 1	What's your name?
Tom	Tom.
Barista 1	Dom. A tea.
Tom	No, I'm Tom, not Dom.

b 🔊 **1.3** Listen and repeat the conversations.

c In pairs, practice the conversations.

2 GRAMMAR verb *be* (singular): *I* and *you*

a Write *I* or *You* in photos 1 and 2.

b 🇬 **p.92 Grammar Bank 1A**

c 🔊 **1.6** Listen and say the contractions.

1 🔊) I am (I'm

_____'m Helen.

_____'re Tom.

3 VOCABULARY numbers 0–10

a 🔊1.7 Listen and check (✓) the correct photo.

b 🅥 p.116 **Vocabulary Bank** Numbers Do Part 1.

c 🔊1.9 Listen and write the numbers.

7 ▯▯▯▯▯▯▯▯▯▯▯

d 🔊1.10 Listen and say the next number.

)) one, two (three

4 PRONUNCIATION
/h/, /aɪ/, and /i/

a 🔊1.11 Listen and repeat the words and sounds.

🏠	house	hi hello Helen
🚲	bike	I'm nice five nine
🌳	tree	meet three tea please

b 🔊1.12 Listen and repeat the sentences.
Hello, Helen!
Hi, I'm Mike.
Three teas, please.

5 SPEAKING

Practice with other students.

Hi, I'm… Are you…?

Yes, I am.
   Nice to meet you.
Nice to meet you.

No, I'm not.
   What's your name?
I'm…
   Nice to meet you.
Nice to meet you.

6 VOCABULARY
days of the week, saying goodbye

a 🔊1.13 Listen and repeat the days of the week.

<u>Mo</u>nday /ˈmʌndeɪ/
<u>Tue</u>sday /ˈtuzdeɪ/
<u>Wed</u>nesday /ˈwɛnzdeɪ/
<u>Thur</u>sday /ˈθɜrzdeɪ/
<u>Fri</u>day /ˈfraɪdeɪ/
<u>Sa</u>turday /ˈsætərdeɪ/
<u>Sun</u>day /ˈsʌndeɪ/

🔍 **Capital letters**
Monday **NOT** ~~monday~~
Friday **NOT** ~~friday~~

b Write the days of the week.

to<u>day</u> = _____   to<u>morrow</u> = _____
the <u>week</u>end = _____ and _____

c Cover **a** and say the days from Monday to Sunday. What days are <u>your</u> English classes?

d 🔊1.14 Listen and repeat.

Goodbye, Tom. See you on Friday.

Bye.

e Say goodbye.   (Bye. See you tomorrow.

WORDS AND PHRASES TO LEARN 1A

p.131 Listen and repeat the words and phrases.

G verb *be* (singular): *he, she, it* **V** countries **P** /ɪ/, /oʊ/, /s/, and /ʃ/

Where's he from?
He's from Brazil.

1 VOCABULARY countries

a 🔊 1.16 Listen to the music. Where's it from? Write 1–5.

☐ Brazil ☐ China [1] Mexico ☐ the US ☐ Turkey

b 🔊 1.17 Listen and check.

c **V** p.117 **Vocabulary Bank** Countries and nationalities
Do Part 1.

d 🔊 1.19 Listen and repeat the conversation. Copy the rhythm.

A **Where** are you **from**?
B I'm from **Li**ma.
A **Where's** **Li**ma?
B It's in **Pe**ru.

e Practice the conversation with your city and country.

f **C** **Communication** Where is it? **A** p.78 **B** p.82 Ask and answer questions about cities and countries.

2 GRAMMAR verb *be* (singular): *he, she, it*

a 🔊 1.20 Listen to the conversation. Write the countries.

A Wow! Caetano Veloso!
B Where's he from?
A He's from _____.
B Is Lila Downs from _____, too?
A No, she isn't. She's from _____.
B Is she good?
A Yes, she is. Very good.

b 🔊 1.21 Listen again and repeat.

c In pairs, practice the conversation.

d Match the words with the photos.

☐ she
☐ it
☐ he

1 2 3

e Complete the chart for *be* (singular).

➕	➖
I am = I'm	I am not = I'm not
you are = you're	you are not = you aren't
he is = he____	he is not = he ____
she is = she____	she is not = she ____
it is = it____	it is not = it ____

f **G** p.92 **Grammar Bank 1B**

WORLD MUSIC FESTIVAL
June 18–19

FRIDAY 18
Caetano Veloso

SATURDAY 19
Lila Downs

ALSO APPEARING
Elena Trona
Mercedes Peón
Gaye Su Akyol
Sergio Mendoza
Ken Yates
Rebelution

3 PRONUNCIATION /ɪ/, /oʊ/, /s/, and /ʃ/

a 🔊 1.25 Listen and repeat the words and sounds.

🐟	fish	it six isn't Brazil England
☎	phone	no don't photo Mexico know
🐍	snake	say seven city nice
🚿	shower	she English

b 🔊 1.26 Listen and repeat the sentences.

It's six in Mexico.   It's a nice city.
I don't know.   She speaks English.

4 LISTENING & SPEAKING

a 🔊 1.27 Listen to the difference between *he* and *she*.

1 a Is he from Vietnam?   b Is she from Vietnam?
2 a He's from Turkey.   b She's from Turkey.
3 a Where's he from?   b Where's she from?
4 a He's nice.   b She's nice.
5 a Where is he?   b Where is she?

b Practice saying sentences a and b.

c 🔊 1.28 Listen and check (✓) the sentence you hear in **a**.

d 🔊 1.29 Listen and write six sentences or questions.

1 *He's from Vietnam.*

e Look at the photos. Ask and answer questions with a partner about the artists or instruments.

Where's he from?) (*He's from the US.*

Where's she from?) (*She's from Turkey.*

Where's it from?) (*It's from China.*

f 🔊 1.30 Listen and check.

g Test your partner. Point to a photo and ask a question with *Is he / she / it from…?*

Number two. Is she from Japan?)

(*No, she isn't. She's from China.*

WORDS AND PHRASES TO LEARN 1B

p.131 Listen and repeat the words and phrases.

Go online to review the lesson

Practical English How do you spell it?

checking into a hotel, booking a table   **V** the classroom   **P** the alphabet

1 THE ALPHABET

a ◀) 1.32 Listen to the alphabet. Repeat the letters.

Aa Bb Cc Dd
Ee Ff Gg Hh
Ii Jj Kk Ll
Mm Nn Oo Pp
Qq Rr Ss Tt
Uu Vv Ww
Xx Yy Zz

b ◀) 1.33 Listen and repeat the words, sounds, and letters.

🌳	tree	B C D E G P T V Z
🥚	egg	F L M N S X
🚂	train	A H J K

c ◀) 1.34 Listen to the difference between the letters.

1 E A		7 G J
2 E I		8 K Q
3 U W		9 M N
4 Y I		10 S C
5 B P		11 D T
6 B V		12 W V

d ◀) 1.35 Listen. Circle the letter you hear in **c**.

e ◀) 1.36 Look at the photos. How do you say the letters? Listen and check.

f ⓒ **Communication** Hit the ships **A** p.78 **B** p.82 Play a game with numbers and letters.

2 VOCABULARY the classroom

a ◀) 1.37 Listen and complete the conversation with the words from the list.

Book   English   spell   What

Student	¹_____'s *libro* in ²_____?
Teacher	³_____.
Student	How do you ⁴_____ it?
Teacher	B-O-O-K.

b ⓥ p.118 **Vocabulary Bank** The classroom

c Complete the conversations.

1 **Teacher** _____ your books, please. _____ to page 7.
  Student _____, can you _____ that, please?
  Teacher Go to page 7.

2 **Student** _____ me. _____ do you spell "birthday"?
  Teacher B-I-R-T-H-D-A-Y.

3 **Student** _____ I'm late.
  Teacher That's OK. Sit _____, please.

d ◀) 1.40 Listen and check.

e In pairs, practice the conversations in **c**.

f ◀) 1.41 Listen and do the actions.

1 ◀)) *Stand up.*

3 ▶ CHECKING INTO A HOTEL

a ◀)1.42 Watch or listen to Rob. (Circle) a or b.

1 Rob is from _____.
  a the UK
  b the US
2 He's _____.
  a an artist
  b a journalist
3 He's in Poland _____.
  a on vacation
  b for work

b ◀)1.43 Watch or listen and order the sentences.

7	W-A-L-K-E-R.
	My name's Rob Walker. I have a reservation.
	Sorry?
1	Hello.
	How do you spell it?
	Walker.
	Sorry, what's your surname?
	Thank you. OK, Mr. Walker. You're in room 321.
	Good afternoon.
	W-A-L-K-E-R.
	Thanks.

> 🔍 **Names**
> **name**   Rob Walker
> **first name**   Rob
> **surname (or last name)**   Walker

c ◀)1.44 Watch or listen and repeat the conversation.

d In pairs, role-play the conversation. Use <u>your</u> name and last name.

> 🔍 **Greetings**
> Good <u>morn</u>ing   » 12:00
> Good <u>after</u>noon   12:00 » 6:00 p.m.
> Good <u>eve</u>ning   6:00 p.m. »

4 ▶ BOOKING A TABLE

a ◀)1.45 Watch or listen to Jenny. (Circle) a or b.
1 Jenny's from _____.
  a the US
  b the UK
2 _____ is her birthday.
  a Today
  b Tomorrow
3 Locanda Verde is a _____.
  a restaurant
  b club

b ◀)1.46 Watch or listen and complete the information.

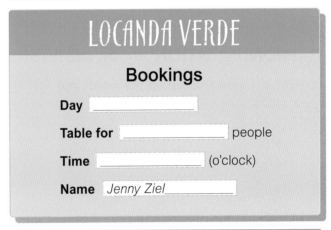

LOCANDA VERDE

Bookings

Day _____
Table for _____ people
Time _____ (o'clock)
Name *Jenny Ziel_____*

> 🔍 **American and British English**
> *vacation* = American English
> *holiday* = British English
>
> *last name* = American English
> *surname* = British English
>
> Z (zee /zi/) = American English
> Z (zed /zɛd/) = British English

5 USEFUL PHRASES

◀)1.47 Listen and repeat the useful phrases.

I have a reservation.	Good morning.
How do you spell it?	How can I help you?
Sorry?	A table for tomorrow, please.
Thank you.	That's right.

 Go online to watch the video and review the lesson

2A Are you on vacation?

> Are you American?
>
> No, we aren't. We're from Canada.

G verb *be* (plural): *we, you, they* | **V** nationalities | **P** /dʒ/, /tʃ/, and /ʃ/

1 VOCABULARY nationalities

a Look at the photos and circle the nationality words.

b Write the countries for each photo.

1 *Turkey*   2 _____

3 _____   4 _____

c **V** p.117 **Vocabulary Bank** Countries and nationalities Do Part 2.

2 PRONUNCIATION /dʒ/, /tʃ/, and /ʃ/

a ◖2.2 Listen and repeat the words and sounds.

	jazz	Japan Argentina
	chess	Chinese Chilean
	shower	Spanish Turkish

> 🔍 Sounds
> The letter *j* = /dʒ/, e.g., **J**apan /dʒəˈpæn/.
> The letter *g* = /dʒ/, e.g., Ar**g**entina /ɑrdʒənˈtinə/ or /g/, e.g., **g**o /goʊ/.

b ◖2.3 Listen and repeat the sentences.
He isn't from Argentina, he's Japanese.
It isn't Chilean. It's Chinese.
She isn't Spanish, she's Turkish.

c ◖2.4 Listen. Say the nationality.

1 ⟩ I'm from China. ⟮ *He's Chinese.*

2 ⟩ I'm from Spain. ⟮ *She's Spanish.*

3 GRAMMAR verb *be* (plural): *we, you, they*

a Read the conversation. Complete it with words from the list.

American ~~are~~ aren't Canadian I'm meet sit Thanks

Jessica Excuse me. Are these seats free?
Max Yes, they ¹ *are*. Please ² _____ down.
Jessica ³ _____. I'm Jessica. Hi.
Jim And ⁴ _____ Jim.
Max Are you ⁵ _____?
Jessica No, we ⁶ _____. We're from the UK.
Max Oh, OK! We're ⁷ _____. I'm Max.
Rachel And I'm Rachel.
Jim Nice to ⁸ _____ you.

b ◖2.5 Listen and check. Then complete the chart.

be (plural)	
+	**−**
we are = we *'re*	we are not = we *aren't*
you are = you _____	you are not = you _____
they are = they _____	they are not = they _____

c **G** p.94 **Grammar Bank 2A**

d ◖2.9 Listen. Ask the questions.

1 ⟩ You're Chinese. ⟮ *Are you Chinese?*

2 ⟩ We're late. ⟮ *Are we late?*

4 READING & LISTENING

a 🔊 2.10 Read and listen to the conversation. Then number the pictures 1–5.

Jessica	Where in the US are you from?
Max	We're from here, from Chicago.
Jim	Chicago's a beautiful city!
Rachel	Yes, it is. Are you on vacation?
Jim	No, we aren't. We're here on business. But today's a free day.
Jessica	Yes, we're tourists today! Ooh. What's that?
Jim	Oh… Are they your dogs?
Max	Yes, they are. Sit. Sit!
Jessica	They're very nice. But I'm not very good with dogs.
Jim	Look – a free table. Over there.
Jessica	Nice to meet you. Have a nice day.
Max	Thanks. Nice to meet you, too.
Rachel	Bye. Good dogs, good dogs.

A

B

C

D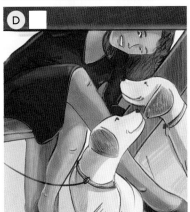

E

b Read the conversation again. Write short answers.

1 Are Rachel and Max from Canada?
No, _____.

2 Are Jessica and Jim on business?
_____

3 Is today a free day for Jessica and Jim?
_____

4 Is Jessica good with dogs?
_____

c 🔊 2.11 Listen and complete the phrases.

1 Excuse me. Are these seats _____?
2 Are you on _____?
3 We're here on _____.
4 What's _____?
5 Have a nice _____!
6 Nice to meet you, _____.

d In groups of four, practice the conversations in **3a** and **4a**.

5 SPEAKING

a Ask and answer the questions with a partner.

1

2

3

4

1 Is Shawn Mendes Canadian?
(Yes, he is. / No, he isn't. / I don't know.
2 Are Chow Chow dogs Mexican?
3 Is Samsung Korean?
4 Is Emma Watson American?

b 🌐 **Communication** Is sushi Chinese?
A p.78 **B** p.82 Ask and answer about different nationalities.

WORDS AND PHRASES TO LEARN 2A

p.131 Listen and repeat the words and phrases.

Go online to review the lesson

That's my bus!

What's your cell phone number?

It's 617-555-8953.

1 READING & LISTENING

a 🔊2.13 Read and listen to the conversation. Then complete the information on the card.

CARNET INTERNACIONAL DE ESTUDIANTE
INTERNATIONAL STUDENT IDENTITY CARD
Name _____ Martínez
Nationality _____
Age _____

Pia	Who's he?
Lin	He's Alex. He's in my class.
Pia	Where's he from?
Lin	He's from Mexico.
Pia	How old is he?
Lin	He's 22, I think.
Pia	He's very good-looking!

b 🔊2.14 Listen and complete the conversation.

Lin	Hi, Pia. How are you?
Pia	Hi, Lin. I'm fine, and you?
Lin	I'm fine, too. This is Alex. He's in my ¹_____. Alex, this is Pia.
Pia	Hi, Alex!
Alex	Hi. ²_____ class are you in?

Lin	That's my bus! Bye. See you ³_____!
Alex	Bye. ⁴_____ are you from, Pia?
Pia	I'm from ⁵_____. This is my bus stop. Bye, Alex. Nice to meet you.
Alex	Nice to meet you, too, Pia. What's your cell ⁶_____ number?
Pia	Sorry, my bus… It's 617-55…!

c 🔊2.15 Listen and repeat the conversation. Then practice it in groups of three.

2 GRAMMAR Wh- and How questions with be

a 🔊2.16 Listen and repeat the question words.

How   What   Where   Who

b Complete the chart with question words from **a**.

1	A *Where* are you from?	B I'm from China.
2	A _____ are you?	B Fine, thanks.
3	A _____'s he?	B He's a friend.
4	A _____'s your name?	B Molly.
5	A _____'s Alberta?	B It's in Canada.
6	A _____ old are you?	B 26.
7	A _____'s your cell phone number?	B 617-555-6879.

c 🔊2.17 Listen and check.

d **G** p.94 Grammar Bank 2B

e Cover the questions in the chart in **b** and look at the answers. Say the questions.

3 VOCABULARY phone numbers, numbers 11–100

a ◀)) 2.19 Listen and complete the phone number.

2 [ ] 2 - [ ] 5 - 0 [ ] [ ]

b ◀)) 2.20 Practice saying these phone numbers. Listen and check.

1 608-5713
2 845-7902
3 231-504-0206

c Ask and answer with a partner. Write the number.

(*What's your phone number?*

d Ⓥ p.116 Vocabulary Bank Numbers Do Part 2.

e ◀)) 2.23 Listen and write the numbers.

15

f Play *Buzz*.

4 PRONUNCIATION & LISTENING understanding numbers

a ◀)) 2.24 Listen to the difference between the numbers.

1 a 13   b 30   5 a 17   b 70
2 a 14   b 40   6 a 18   b 80
3 a 15   b 50   7 a 19   b 90
4 a 16   b 60

b ◀)) 2.25 Listen. Which number do you hear? Circle a or b in a. Then practice saying all the numbers.

c ◀)) 2.26 Listen to the conversations. Number the questions 1–4.

[ ] What's your address?   [ ] What's your email?
[ ] How old are you?   [ ] What's your cell phone number?

d Listen again and write the numbers in the answers.

1 ☎ _____
2 _____ Oak Street
3 Age: _____
4 james_____@geemail.com

> 🔍 Email addresses
> @ = at   . = dot

5 WRITING & SPEAKING

a Ⓦ p.86 Writing A form Complete an online form.

b Ⓒ Communication Personal information A p.79 B p.83 Interview your partner.

6 ▶ VIDEO LISTENING Meet the students

a Watch the video *Meet the students*. Is it a nice school?

b Watch again. Circle the correct answer.

1 San Francisco is on the *east / west* coast of the United States.
2 San Francisco *is / isn't* famous for cable cars.
3 Rike and Hyeongwoo are *teachers / students*.
4 Hyeongwoo is *23 / 26* years old.
5 His teacher is *Stephen / Laura*.
6 Rike is *Brazilian / Chilean*.
7 Laura is a good *teacher / student*.
8 Their student house *is / isn't* near the school.

c Watch some extracts from the video. Complete the sentences with words from the list.

bedrooms   big   cafeteria   computer room
kitchen   small   yard

1 It's a _____ school with about 350 students.
2 His class is _____, with only five students.
3 …they're in the _____…or here in the _____.
4 It's a big house with five _____, a _____, and a _____.

WORDS AND PHRASES TO LEARN 2B

p.131 Listen and repeat the words and phrases.

GRAMMAR

Circle a or b.

_____'s your name?
a Who b (What)

1 _____ you from Peru?
a Are b Is

2 _____ Lisa. I'm Marisa.
a Am not b I'm not

3 Hi, Mark! _____ in my class.
a You b You're

4 A _____ from?
B I'm from Saudi Arabia.
a Where are you b Where you are

5 A Where's Toronto?
B _____ in Canada.
a Is b It's

6 A Is John married?
B No, _____.
a he isn't b she isn't

7 A _____ English?
B No, she's American.
a She's b Is she

8 They _____ Spanish. They're Mexican.
a aren't b not

9 A Are you on vacation?
B No, _____ here on business.
a we're b we

10 Ana and Julia are from Recife. _____ Brazilian.
a She's b They're

11 A _____ Abe and Keiko Japanese?
B Yes, they're from Tokyo.
a Are b Is

12 A How old _____?
B I'm 19.
a you are b are you

13 A _____ are you?
B Fine, thanks. And you?
a How b Who

14 A _____ address?
B It's 304 Main Street.
a What your b What's your

15 A How _____ your last name?
B G-A-R-C-I-A.
a you spell b do you spell

VOCABULARY

a Complete the chart.

Country	Nationality
China	Chinese
Turkey	1 _____
2 _____	Saudi
the United States	3 _____
4 _____	English
5 _____	Brazilian
Japan	6 _____

b Write the next number or word.

one, two, *three*
1 zero, one, _____
2 five, six, _____
3 eleven, twelve, _____
4 nineteen, twenty, _____
5 Tuesday, Wednesday, _____
6 Friday, Saturday, _____

c Complete the words.

Where are you **fr***om*?
1 Good morning. **O**_____ your books, please. Page 19.
2 A **S**_____ I'm late.
  B OK. Sit **d**_____.
3 A What's the answer to number 10?
  B I don't **kn**_____.
4 A Excuse **m**_____, **wh**_____ *plato* in English?
  B Plate.
  A Can you **r**_____ that, please?
  B Yes. Plate.
5 A What's your phone **n**_____?
  B 555-8942.
  A Thanks. What's your **e**_____?
  B It's tom@hotmail.com.

d Write the things in the classroom.

a dictionary

1 _____ 2 _____ 3 _____ 4 _____

PRONUNCIATION

a Write the words for the sound pictures.

bike	bike	3	
1		4	
2		5	

b 🅿 p.134–5 **Sound Bank** Look at more words with the sounds in **a**, and these sounds:

Practice saying the example words.

c Underline the stressed syllable.

Sa|tur|day
1 Chi|nese
2 fif|ty
3 fif|teen
4 to|morr|ow
5 Ar|gen|ti|ni|an

CAN YOU understand this text?

Read the profiles and complete the chart for Mark, Bianca, and Jacek. Then add information about you.

I'm **Mark Davis**. I'm from Seattle in the US. I'm a teacher. I'm twenty-eight and I'm single.

I'm **Bianca Costa**. I'm from Rio in Brazil. I'm twenty. I'm single and I'm a student.

I'm **Roger Ford**. I'm forty. I'm from Vancouver in Canada. I'm married, with two children. I'm a doctor.

First name	Mark	Bianca	Roger	_____ (= you)
Last name				
Age	28			
Nationality				
Marital status		single		
Occupation			doctor	

▶ CAN YOU understand these people?

🔊2.28 Watch or listen and answer the questions.

1 — 2 Brian 3 Richard 4 Rytis 5 Christopher

1 The woman's name is _____.
   a Gayna
   b Jeina
   c Jayna
2 Brian is from _____.
   a New York
   b California
   c Texas
3 Richard is _____ years old.
   a 46
   b 56
   c 66
4 Rytis's phone number is _____.
   a 347-222-1289
   b 374-222-1289
   c 247-222-2198
5 Christopher's email address is _____.
   a cyoon123it@yahoo.com
   b chrisyoon@yahoo.com
   c cyoonit123@yahoo.com

CAN YOU say this in English?

Check (✓) the boxes.

Can you...?	Yes, I can.
1 say your name and where you are from	☐
2 ask where other people are from	☐
3 spell your name	☐
4 count from 0 to 100	☐
5 ask for and give personal information, e.g., name, address, age, etc.	☐
6 say your phone number	☐
7 use and understand classroom language	☐
8 check into a hotel	☐
9 book a table at a restaurant	☐

🔵 **Go online** to watch the video, review Files 1 & 2, and check your progress

> Is it an ID card?
> No, it's a credit card.

G singular and plural nouns, a / an **V** small things **P** /z/ and /s/, plural endings

1 VOCABULARY small things

a What are the four things? Can you remember?

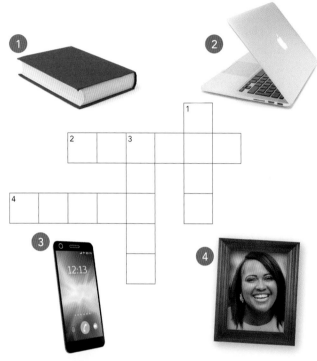

b **V** p.119 **Vocabulary Bank** Small things

2 GRAMMAR singular and plural nouns, a / an

a Read the list. What do you think are the top four things?

Oh no! Where's my phone?

Every day people all over the world say, "Oh no! Where's my...?" The top eight things that people look for are (not in the correct order):

- pens and pencils
- glasses and sunglasses
- keys (house keys and car keys)
- wallets and change purses
- bank cards
- cell phones
- umbrellas
- phone chargers

b 🔊 3.2 Listen and number the things 1–8 in the list in **a**. Is this order true for <u>you</u>?

(*For me, number one is my glasses.*

c Look at the photos. Complete the chart.

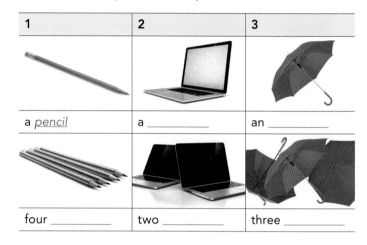

1	2	3
a *pencil*	a _____	an _____
four _____	two _____	three _____

d **G** p.96 **Grammar Bank 3A**

e **C** **Communication** Memory game p.81 Remember the things in the photo.

3 PRONUNCIATION /z/ and /s/, plural endings

a 🔊 3.5 Listen and repeat the words and sound.

zebra	zero Brazil is he's

b 🔊 3.6 Listen and repeat the plural words and sounds.

🦓	bags phones keys pens
🐍	books coats passports tablets
/ɪz/	watches glasses pieces change purses

c 🔊 3.7 Listen. Say the plural.

1 🔊 *It's a photo.* (*They're photos.*

4 LISTENING

a ◎ 3.8 Listen to five situations. Number the photos 1–5.

b Listen again. Write the small things for each situation.

1 _____
2 _____
3 _____
4 _____
5 _____

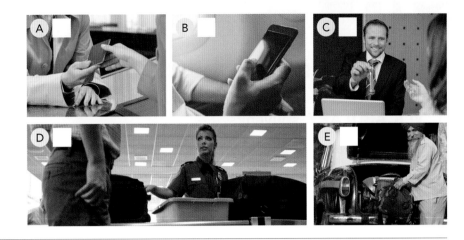

5 SPEAKING

a Look at the photos. What are the things? Work with a partner. **A** ask **B** about photo 1. **B** ask **A** about photo 2. Continue with the other photos.

What is it?) (*(I think) it's a / an...*

What are they?) (*(I think) they're...*
(*I don't know.*

b What's in your bag or pocket? Check (✓) the things.

▨ a book
▨ a credit card
▨ glasses
▨ an ID card
▨ keys
▨ a pen
▨ a pencil
▨ a phone
▨ a photo
▨ a change purse
▨ an umbrella
▨ a wallet

c Now tell a partner.

(*In my bag, I have a book, keys, a pen...*

d What other things do you have in your bag or pocket? Ask your teacher.

(*What's...in English? How do you spell it?*

WORDS AND PHRASES TO LEARN 3A

p.131 Listen and repeat the words and phrases.

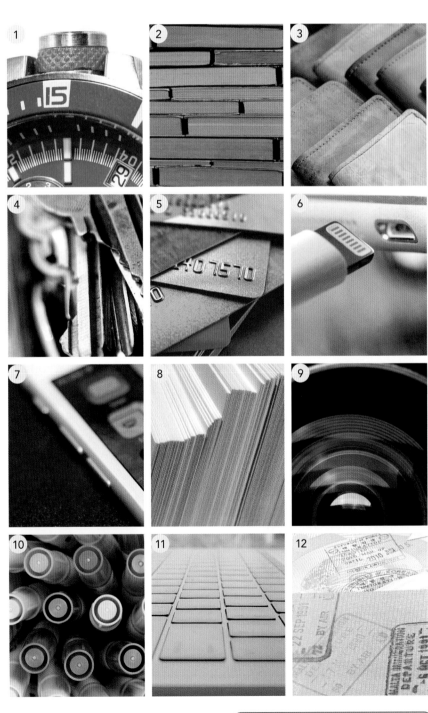

Go online to review the lesson

G this / that / these / those **V** souvenirs **P** /ð/, sentence rhythm

What are those?

They're key chains.

1 VOCABULARY souvenirs

a 🔊 3.10 Look at the eight things. Listen and repeat the words.

1 a cap /kæp/

2 a map /mæp/

3 a <u>post</u>card /ˈpoʊstkɑrd/

4 a key chain /ˈki tʃeɪn/

5 a mug /mʌg/

6 <u>sun</u>glasses /ˈsʌnglæsəz/

7 a toy /tɔɪ/

8 a <u>T</u>-shirt /ˈti ʃɜrt/

b Cover the words and photos and look at the souvenir stand. Say the souvenirs 1–8.

c What are typical souvenirs in <u>your</u> country?

2 LISTENING

a 🔊 3.11 Listen and complete the conversation with numbers.

Woman	Excuse me. What are those?
Man	They're caps.
Woman	How much are they?
Man	They're ¹ $_____.

Woman	And how much are these key chains?
Man	They're ² $_____.
Woman	And this mug?
Man	³ $_____.

Woman	Is that a Yankees T-shirt?
Man	No, it's a Mets T-shirt.
Woman	How much is it?
Man	⁴ $_____.
Woman	Oh...no. Thank you. Bye.

b 🔊 3.12 Listen and repeat the conversation in **a**. Then practice with a partner.

c 🔊 3.13 Listen. What does the woman buy?

3 GRAMMAR *this / that / these / those*

a Read the conversation in **2** again. Complete the chart with the highlighted words.

	here	there
singular	*this*	
plural		

b 🅖 p.96 Grammar Bank 3B

4 PRONUNCIATION & SPEAKING
/ð/, sentence rhythm

a 🔊 3.15 Listen and repeat the words and sound.

👶 mother	this that these those the they

b 🔊 3.16 Listen and complete the conversations with words and numbers.

1 How much is this _____?
  It's $_____.
2 How much is that _____?
  It's $_____.
3 How much are these _____?
  They're $_____.
4 How much are those _____?
  They're $_____.
5 Two _____, please.
  That's $_____.

c Listen again. Then repeat the conversations. Copy the rhythm.

d 🅒 **Communication** How much are these watches? A p.79 B p.83 Role-play conversations.

WORDS AND PHRASES TO LEARN 3B

p.131 Listen and repeat the words and phrases.

🔵 Go online to review the lesson

Practical English Can I have an orang

understanding prices, buying lunch   **P** /ʊr/, /s/, and /k/

1 UNDERSTANDING PRICES

a 🔊 3.18 Listen and repeat.

ten **pounds**

fifty **pence** (fifty **p**)

ten **euros**

fifty **cents**

ten **dollars**

twenty-five **cents**

b Match the prices and words.

1	H	£12.75	A thirteen dollars and twenty-five cents
2		€15.99	B eighty cents
3		$50.19	C five pounds thirty-five
4		£5.35	D fifteen euros ninety-nine
5		$13.25	E sixty pence
6		€3.20	F fifty dollars and nineteen cents
7		€0.25	G three euros twenty
8		£1.50	H twenty pounds seventy-five (struck through: twelve pounds seventy-five)
9		60p	I one pound fifty
10		$0.80	J twenty-five cents

c 🔊 3.19 Listen and check. Then listen and repeat.

d Cover the words and look at the prices. Practice saying them.

e 🔊 3.20 Listen to four conversations. How much is it? Circle the correct price.

1	newspaper:	$2.50	$2.15
2	umbrella:	€15	€50
3	memory card:	$4.99	$9.49
4	train ticket:	£13.20	£30.20

2 PRONUNCIATION /ʊr/, /s/, and /k/

🔊 3.21 Listen and repeat the words and sounds.

🧑	tourist	euro Europe sure tour
🐍	snake	cent city pence price
🔑	key	coffee Canada credit card

> 🔍 The letter *c*
> *c* = /s/ before *e*, *i*, and *y*, e.g., *cent*, *city*.
> *c* = /k/ before other letters, e.g., *coffee*.

3 ▶ BUYING LUNCH

a 🔊 3.22 Read the menu. Then listen and repeat the food, drinks, and prices.

b Practice with a partner. Ask the prices on the menu.

How much is a tuna sandwich?   *£4.15.*

uice, please?

c 🔊 **3.23** Watch or listen to Rob in a London pub. Check (✓) the things he orders on the menu in **a**.

d Watch or listen again and complete the conversation.

Server	Who's next?
Rob	Can I have a ¹_____ sandwich, please?
Server	Anything else?
Rob	And a ²_____, please.
Server	Ice and lemon?
Rob	³_____, thanks.
Server	There you go.
Rob	Thanks. How much is it?
Server	⁴_____.
Rob	Here you ⁵_____.
Server	Thanks. Here's your change.

e 🔊 **3.24** Watch or listen and repeat. Then practice the conversation with a partner.

f Now role-play the conversation in pairs. **A** You are the server. **B** Order food and a drink. Then change roles.

g 🔊 **3.25** Watch or listen to Jenny and her friend Amy in a New York deli. How much is Jenny's lunch?

h Watch or listen again. What do they have? Complete the chart.

Jenny	
Amy	

4 USEFUL PHRASES

🔊 **3.26** Listen and repeat the useful phrases.

Can I have a cheese sandwich, please?	Here you are.
Anything else?	Here's your change.
And a Coke, please.	I'm fine, too.
Ice and lemon?	Wait for me.
No, thanks.	Sure!
How much is it?	Great idea.

4A Meet the family

Who's Victoria?

She's my boyfriend's sister.

G possessive adjectives, possessive 's **V** people and family **P** /ʌ/, /æ/, and /ə/

1 VOCABULARY people and family

a Look at the photos. Match the words to people 1–4.

| a boy | a girl | a man | a woman |

b 🔊 4.1 Listen and check.

c Ⓥ p.120 **Vocabulary Bank** People and family

2 PRONUNCIATION /ʌ/, /æ/, and /ə/

a 🔊 4.5 Listen and repeat the words and sounds.

↑	up	husband Sunday son mother brother
	cat	man family bag thanks that
	computer	woman children welcome parent

🔍 /ə/
/ə/ is a very common vowel sound in syllables that <u>aren't</u> stressed, e.g., w<u>o</u>man, w<u>el</u>come.

b 🔊 4.6 Listen and repeat. Practice the sentences.
"Is Justin your husband?"   "No, he's my brother."
I have a big family. That's my grandfather.
The man and woman over there are my grandparents.

3 GRAMMAR possessive adjectives, possessive 's

a 🔊 4.7 Read and listen to the conversation on p.25. Do you think Sarah is a) a friend of the family b) a new babysitter?

b Look at photo A. Point to the people and say their names.

(He's Mark.

c Read and listen again. Then complete the chart with a highlighted phrase.

I	my husband
you	
he	
she	
it	
we	our children
you (plural)	
they	

d Read Part B again. Complete the sentences.
1 The name of the restaurant is _____ Café.
2 My _____ phone number is there, too.

e 🔊 4.8 Listen. Do you think Sarah is a good babysitter?

f Ⓖ p.98 **Grammar Bank 4A**

g Point to people in the classroom. What are their names?

(What's his name?
   (What's her name?

h Look at photo A on p.25. With a partner, say as much as you can about each person.

(His name's Oliver. He's Maria's son / Emma's brother.

Maria	Hi, Sarah! Come in.
Sarah	Thanks.
Maria	This is my husband, Mark.
Mark	Hello.
Sarah	Hi.
Maria	And these are our children.
Children	Hello!
Sarah	What are their names?
Maria	Her name's Emma, and his name's Oliver.
Emma	And this is our cat.
Sarah	Oh, cute! What's its name?
Emma	*Her* name is Princess. She's a girl.
Sarah	Oh, sorry.

Maria	The name of the restaurant is Marc's Café. The phone number's on the table over there.
Sarah	Great, thanks.
Maria	And my husband's phone number is there, too.
Sarah	OK. And your number is in my phone.
Maria	Now, children. Sarah is your babysitter. Be good.
Children	OK, Mom.

4 LISTENING

See you soon! Jerry & Mia
Shira,

Love, Hayley

Love, Buddy

Have a fantastic day! Paul

Happy birthday!

22! WoW! Love Nicole + John

Dear Carly,
Happy Birthday

Love,
Mom and Dad

a 🔊 4.11 Carly is in Mexico with her friend Marina. It's her birthday. Look at her birthday card and listen. Who are the people?

1 Paul is *Carly*'s *brother*.
2 Hayley is _____'s _____.
3 Shira is _____'s _____.
4 Nicole is _____'s _____.
5 John is _____'s _____.

b Listen again. Answer the questions.

1 How old are Paul and Nicole?
2 Who are Mia and Buddy?

5 SPEAKING & WRITING

a Work with a partner:

A and **B** write the names of six people (your family or friends) on a piece of paper.

A give your piece of paper to **B**. **B** give your piece of paper to **A**.

A ask **B** about his / her people. **B** ask **A** about his / her people.

Who's Marco? *He's my sister's husband.*

b 🅦 p.86 Writing A post about a photo
Write about a photo of your family.

WORDS AND PHRASES TO LEARN 4A

p.131 Listen and repeat the words and phrases.

4B The perfect car

G adjectives | **V** colors and common adjectives | **P** /ɑr/ and /ɔr/, linking

> Is it a good car?
> No, it isn't. It's small and very slow.

1 LISTENING & VOCABULARY
colors and common adjectives

a Take the quiz with a partner. Match the logos to the cars. What nationality are they?

1 is a Chevrolet. I think it's American. Or English.

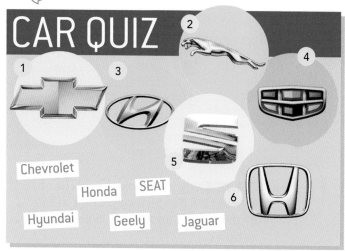

CAR QUIZ

Chevrolet
Honda   SEAT
Hyundai   Geely   Jaguar

b ◄))4.13 Listen and check.

c ◄))4.14 Now look at the picture and listen to the conversation. Which car is perfect for the woman…?

   a in her opinion   b in her son's opinion

d Read the conversation. Write the highlighted words under the two cars.

Salesperson	Is the car for you?
Man	No, it's for my mother.
Woman	Yes, it's for me.
Salesperson	For you, ma'am? Well, what about this blue car here? It's small and it's easy to park.
Man	Yes, Mom, it's perfect for you.
Woman	But it's very slow. And it's ugly.
Salesperson	It's an electric car, ma'am. Very eco-friendly. They're good cars.
Woman	I prefer…this red car.
Man	But Mom, it's a sports car! It's very fast. And it's very expensive.
Woman	Yes, but it's my money. It's a beautiful car and I love it! How much is it?
Salesperson	Come with me, ma'am.
Man	Mom! …

e ◄))4.15 Listen and repeat the conversation. Then practice it in groups of three.

f **V** p.121 **Vocabulary Bank** Adjectives

g With a partner, talk about <u>your</u> car or your family's car.

My car is a Chevrolet Cruze. It's American. It's small and it's green. It isn't very fast.

2 GRAMMAR adjectives

a (Circle) a or b.

1 a It's a beautiful car.
   b It's a car beautiful.
2 a They're goods cars.
   b They're good cars.

b **G** p.98 **Grammar Bank 4B**

c ◀))4.20 Listen and say the plural.

1)) *an American car* (*American cars*

3 PRONUNCIATION /ɑr/ and /ɔr/, linking

a ◀))4.21 Listen and repeat the words and sounds.

	car	large park are tomorrow
	horse	short sport orange door

b ◀))4.22 Listen. Practice the phrases.

a big umbrella   an old man
a short email   an orange coat
brown eggs   an expensive watch

c ◀))4.23 Listen and write five phrases.

d With a partner, look at the photos from
Vocabulary Bank Adjectives and make sentences.

(*It's a black bag.* (*They're blue keys.*

4 SPEAKING

Talk in small groups.

I prefer small cities.) (**Me too.** (*I prefer big cities.*

big small
cities

Japanese Mexican
food

British American
movies

cheap expensive
restaurants

old new
houses

long short
books

big small
dogs

black and white color
photos

5 ▶ VIDEO LISTENING Beaulieu Motor Museum

a Watch the video *Beaulieu Motor Museum.* Which is your
favorite car?

b Watch again. Mark the sentences **T** (true) or **F** (false).

1 Beaulieu is a small village.
2 It isn't famous.
3 The National Motor Museum is 52 years old.
4 The host's favorite car is the Bluebird.
5 The Ferrari Dino is 14 years old.
6 The Ford Anglia is an American car.
7 It's famous because it's in the Star Wars movies.
8 The National Motor Museum has motorcycles, too.

c Do you think it's an interesting museum?

WORDS AND PHRASES TO LEARN 4B

p.131 Listen and repeat the words and phrases.

Go online to watch the video and review the lesson

GRAMMAR

Circle a or b.

_____'s your name?
a Who   b What

1 Look! It's _____ email from Melanie.
   a an   b a

2 A Where are my sunglasses?   B _____ in your bag.
   a It's   b They're

3 These are nice _____.
   a watchs   b watches

4 Kyoto and Osaka are two important _____ in Japan.
   a citys   b cities

5 A What's _____?
   B It's a key chain.
   a this   b these

6 How much are _____ T-shirts?
   a those   b that

7 Look at _____ house over there. It's beautiful.
   a this   b that

8 _____ my friend, Tom.
   a It is   b This is

9 He's Mexican. _____ name is Miguel.
   a His   b Her

10 We're Mr. and Mrs. Brown. _____ son's name is Joe.
   a Our   b Their

11 Justin is _____ brother.
   a Sophies   b Sophie's

12 My _____ is Amanda.
   a name's wife   b wife's name

13 These chairs are _____.
   a very expensive   b very expensives

14 A Hyundai is a _____.
   a car Korean   b Korean car

15 They're _____.
   a good photos   b goods photos

VOCABULARY

a   Write a / an + the things.

a wallet   1 _____   2 _____

3 _____   4 _____   5 _____

b   Complete the chart.

| 👤 | man | father | 2 _____ | son | 4 _____ | boyfriend |
| 👤 | woman | 1 _____ | wife | 3 _____ | sister | 5 _____ |

c   Write the plural.

mother + father = parents
1 a woman   two _____
2 a child   three _____
3 a man   four _____
4 a person   50 _____

d   Write the colors.

□ white
1 ■ _____   4 ▢ _____
2 ▨ _____   5 ■ _____
3 ▦ _____   6 ▤ _____

e   Write the opposite adjectives.

fast slow
1 big _____   3 long _____
2 expensive _____   4 new _____
                      5 ugly _____

PRONUNCIATION

a   Write the words for the sound pictures.

_____   _____
 bike   3 _____

1 _____   4 _____

2 _____   5 _____

b   🅟 p.134–5 Sound Bank Look at more words with the sounds in a, and these sounds:

Practice saying the example words.

c   Underline the stressed syllable.

um|bre|lla   2 sun|glass|es   4 ex|pen|sive
1 wo|man   3 or|ange   5 si|ster

CAN YOU understand this text?

a Read the two texts and write the people's names in the pictures.

1   2   3   4

My name's Jeremy Fisher and I'm from Vancouver in Canada. I'm married to Anna and I have two children, a son and a daughter. My son's name is Matthew. He's 17. He's tall with dark hair. My daughter's name is Susanna. She's 19. I think my children are good-looking, probably because their mother is beautiful!

1   2   3

My name's Maddie and I'm from Seattle in the US. I'm 22. I have two sisters. Their names are Finn and Stella. Finn is 24. She's good-looking, with long blond hair. She isn't married. Stella is 31 and very different from Finn, but she's good-looking, too. She's married. Her husband's name is Ezra.

b Read again and answer the questions with a sentence.

1 What's Jeremy's last name?

_____

2 Where is he from?

_____

3 What's his son's name?

_____

4 How old is Susanna?

_____

5 What nationality is Maddie?

_____

6 Who is Finn?

_____

7 Is she married?

_____

8 How old is Stella?

_____

CAN YOU understand these people?

◉4.25 Watch or listen and answer the questions.

1 Richard   2 Josh   3 Kieran   4 Debra   5 Daniel

1 What's in Richard's bag?
   a his keys
   b his coat
   c his camera
2 What's in Josh's bag?
   a his phone, charger, and umbrella
   b his notebooks, charger, and laptop
   c his charger, laptop, and books
3 There are ____ people in Kieran's family.
   a 4
   b 5
   c 6
4 A cup of coffee in Debra's local coffee shop is ____.
   a cheap
   b £4
   c $4
5 Daniel's car is ____.
   a small
   b black
   c a Honda

CAN YOU say this in English?

Check (✓) the boxes.

Can you...?	Yes, I can.
1 say what's in your bag	
2 talk about things with *this*, *that*, *these*, and *those*	
3 say who is in your family	
4 introduce somebody	
5 describe cars	
6 ask for things in a café or store	
7 ask about prices	

5A A big breakfast?

We have fruit and cereal for breakfast.

I don't have breakfast. I have a coffee at work.

1 VOCABULARY food and drink

a Re-order the letters to make food and drink words. Match them to photos A–E.

1 ▨ AET _____

2 ▨ ESHECE _____

3 ▨ GRANEO CUJIE _____

4 ▨ WANDCHIS _____

5 ▨ GESG _____

b ◉ 5.1 Listen and check.

c **V** p.122 **Vocabulary Bank** Food and drink

2 READING & SPEAKING

a Look at the photos and read the article and comments. Who thinks breakfast is a) important, b) not important?

b ◉ 5.4 Complete the comments with food and drink words. Then listen and check.

c Read the comments again. Circle the places where they have breakfast. Underline the other words for food and drink.

d Is breakfast important for you? What do you have? Where do you have it?

A good breakfast – is it important?

Is breakfast a very important meal, or not important at all? Scientists and doctors have different opinions: some think that a big breakfast is good for you because you eat less during the day. Others say that if you aren't hungry, don't have breakfast. It's only extra calories!

Is breakfast important for *you*? Send us a photo of your breakfast.

Comments

Ashley, the US
I have breakfast in a great café near my office. I have a ¹**cr**_oissant_ and coffee – an espresso with hot ²**m**_____. Mmmm. I love breakfast! It's my favorite meal.

Paulo, Brazil
I have breakfast at home, but I don't have a big breakfast. I have ³**fr**_____ and ⁴**y**_____, and sometimes toast. It's a healthy breakfast. That's a good thing at the beginning of the day.

Rob, Canada
I don't eat in the morning. I'm not hungry. I just have a ⁵**c**_____ at work. But I have lunch early, at about 11:30.

Sakura, Japan
I really like breakfast. It's an important meal for Japanese people. I have breakfast at home with my family. We have a traditional breakfast. It isn't very different from lunch and dinner. We have ⁶**r**_____, ⁷**f**_____, and miso soup and we drink green tea. We don't drink coffee with a traditional Japanese breakfast.

3 GRAMMAR simple present ⊞ and ⊟: *I, you, we, they*

a Complete the sentences from the comments in **2**.

simple present ⊞ and ⊟
⊞ **Ashley**
1 I _____ breakfast in a great café.
Sakura
2 I really _____ breakfast.
3 We _____ a traditional breakfast.
⊟ **Paulo**
4 I _____ _____ a big breakfast.
Rob
5 I _____ _____ in the morning.
Sakura
6 We _____ _____ coffee with a traditional Japanese breakfast.

b **G** p.100 **Grammar Bank 5A**

c Look at **Vocabulary Bank** Food and drink p.122 Say what you like 🙂 and don't like 🙁.

(*I like fish. I don't like meat.*

4 LISTENING

a ◖ 5.6 Listen to Anna talk about her favorite meal. Complete her column in the chart.

	Anna	Will	Sarah
Favorite meal	dinner	lunch	breakfast
Where?	[1] At _____ or at a _____.	[4] At _____.	[7] Usually at _____. On Wednesdays at a _____.
Food	[2] _____ or _____ and _____.	[5] Different things but with _____.	[8] _____ and an _____. On Wednesdays a _____.
Drink	[3] A cup of _____.	[6] _____ and then a _____.	[9] _____ or _____. On Wednesdays _____.

b ◖ 5.7 Now repeat for Will and Sarah.

c What's <u>your</u> favorite meal of the day?

5 PRONUNCIATION /dʒ/ and /g/

a ◖ 5.8 Listen and repeat the words and sounds.

	jazz	juice vegetables orange
	girl	sugar yogurt eggs

> 🔍 *g* and *j*
> Remember *j* always = /dʒ/. *g* is sometimes /g/ (e.g., su*g*ar) and sometimes /dʒ/ (e.g., oran*g*e), especially before *e*.

b ◖ 5.9 Listen. Practice the sentences.
I'm Jane. I like orange juice and vegetables.
I'm Grace. I have eggs, and coffee with sugar.

6 SPEAKING

a Complete the sentences so they are true about <u>you</u> and people in your country.

Food: you and your country
You
I have breakfast _____. (Where?)
I have _____ for breakfast. (What?)
I have lunch _____. (Where?)
I have dinner with _____. (Who?)
I eat a lot of _____. (What?)
I love _____. (What?)
I don't like _____. (What?)
Your country
People have _____ for breakfast. (What?)
They have a big _____. (lunch / dinner)
They _____ a lot of food from other countries. (eat / don't eat)
They eat a lot of _____. (What?)
They drink a lot of _____. (What?)

b Talk to a partner. Say your first sentence. Then say *What about you?*

I have breakfast at home. What about you?)
(*I have breakfast at home, too.*

7 WRITING

W p.86 **Writing** A comment post Write about your breakfast.

WORDS AND PHRASES TO LEARN 5A

p.131 Listen and repeat the words and phrases.

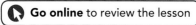 **Go online** to review the lesson

1 GRAMMAR simple present ?: *I, you, we, they*

a 🔊 5.11 Eve, a British woman, and Wendy, an American woman, are on a flight from London to New York. Listen to the conversation and number the pictures 1–4.

1	**Eve**	Do you like the ¹_____?
	Wendy	Yes, I do. It's very good.
	Eve	She's my favorite writer. I love her books.

2	**Eve**	Do you live in ²_____?
	Wendy	No, I don't. I live in London. My husband and I work for a British company.
	Eve	Oh! Do you have ³_____?
	Wendy	No, we don't.
	Eve	I have two sons and a daughter. David and Andrew are in college and Carla's in high school. Look. Here are some photos… This is a photo of our vacation in Barbados. Do you know Barbados?
	Wendy	No, I don't.

3	**Attendant**	Do you want ⁴_____, fish, or pasta?
	Eve	Oh, fish, please.
	Wendy	Pasta for me, please.
	Eve	How's your pasta?
	Wendy	It's OK.
	Eve	This fish isn't very good. Excuse me, I don't like this fish. Can I have the ⁵_____, please?
	Attendant	I'm sorry, ma'am. We're out of pasta.

4	**Eve**	Oh, I need to go to the restroom. Oops, sorry.
	Wendy	Excuse me. What ⁶_____ do we arrive?
	Attendant	In 25 minutes, ma'am.
	Wendy	That's good!

b Read the conversation and complete it with words from the list.

book children meat New York pasta time

c Listen again and check.

d <u>Underline</u> the questions and short answers in parts 1 and 2 of the conversation.

e Ⓖ p.100 **Grammar Bank 5B**

Do you live in New York?

No, I don't. I live in London.

A

B

C

D

2 VOCABULARY common verb phrases 1

a Match the phrases.

1 I love   *d*   a in London.
2 I live   b two sons and a daughter.
3 I work   c for a British company.
4 I want   d her books.
5 I have   e the fish, please.

b Ⓥ **p.123 Vocabulary Bank** Common verb phrases 1

c Write four true sentences about <u>you</u>, two positive and two negative.

I watch CNN.   I don't read a newspaper.

d In pairs, read your sentences to each other. Are any of them the same?

3 LISTENING

a ◑5.15 At the end of her trip, Eve gets a taxi back to the airport. Read sentences 1–10 and look at the **bold** words. Then listen and ⓒircle a or b.

1 a Her flight is from **Newark** airport.
  (b) Her flight is from **JFK**.
2 a The traffic is **bad**.
  b The traffic is **good**.
3 a Eve is from **Manchester**.
  b Eve is from **London**.
4 a The taxi driver is from **New York**.
  b The taxi driver is from **Puerto Rico**.
5 a London is very **cheap**.
  b London is very **expensive**.
6 a The taxi driver has two **sons**.
  b The taxi driver has two **daughters**.
7 a The taxi is **$87.50**.
  b The taxi is **$87.15**.
8 a The taxi driver says "Have a good **day**."
  b The taxi driver says "Have a good **flight**."
9 a Eve **is late**.
  b Eve **isn't late**.
10 a The gate number is **B5**.
  b The gate number is **C5**.

b ◑5.16 Listen to what happens in the airport. Why does Eve say "What a nice surprise!"?

4 PRONUNCIATION & SPEAKING
/w/ and /v/, sentence rhythm and linking

a ◑5.17 Listen and repeat the words and sounds.

🪄	witch	want work when where
🌷	vase	very have live TV

b ◑5.18 Listen. Notice the linked (‿) words.

1 A Do you **live** in a **small house**?
  B No, I **don't**. I **live** in a **big house**.

2 A Do you **have** a **big family**?
  B **Yes**, I **do**. I **have three sisters**.

3 A Do you **watch** a lot of **TV**?
  B No, I **don't**. I **read books**.

c Listen again and repeat. <u>C</u>opy the <u>rhy</u>thm.

d ◑5.19 Now listen and write five sentences.

e Complete 2–10 with a verb from the list.

| drink   eat   go   have   listen   ~~live~~ |
| need   read   speak   watch |

Do you...

1 *live* near here? / in a house or an apartment?
2 _____ brothers and sisters? / a cat or a dog?
3 _____ TV on your phone? / YouTube videos?
4 _____ to pop music? / to classical music?
5 _____ a newspaper? / magazines?
6 _____ meat? / a lot of chocolate?
7 _____ orange juice? / tea?
8 _____ Spanish? / Arabic?
9 _____ a new phone? / a new car?
10 _____ to a gym? / to the movies on weekends?

f Ask and answer questions with a partner.

Do you live near here?   *Yes, I do. I live near the park.*

Do you live in a house or an apartment?
    I live in a small apartment.

WORDS AND PHRASES TO LEARN 5B

p.131 Listen and repeat the words and phrases.

3 Practical English What time is it?

telling the time   **V** the time, saying how you feel   **P** /ɑ/, silent consonants

1 ▶ TELLING THE TIME

a 🔊 5.21 Watch or listen and match the conversations to photos A–C.

1	Rob	I'm tired. What time is it?
	Alan	It's eleven o'clock.
	Rob	I need to go. I have a meeting in Oxford tomorrow morning.
	Alan	One more drink?
	Rob	Oh, OK!
2	Rob	Excuse me. What time is it?
	Woman	It's a quarter to eight. What time's your train?
	Rob	At seven forty-seven.
	Woman	You need to hurry! You only have two minutes.
	Rob	Thanks!
3	Rob	Hello. I'm Rob Walker. I'm sorry I'm late.
	Man	You're an hour late. It's half past ten.
	Rob	I know. I'm really sorry.

b 🔊 5.22 Watch or listen and repeat the conversations in **a**. Then practice them with a partner.

c Cover the conversations and look at the clocks in photos A–C. What time is it?

2 VOCABULARY the time

a 🔊 5.23 Listen and repeat the times.

It's three o'clock.   It's five after three.   It's ten after three.   It's (a) quarter after three.

It's twenty after three.   It's twenty-five after three.   It's three-thirty.   It's twenty-five to four.

It's twenty to four.   It's (a) quarter to four.   It's ten to four.   It's five to four.

b Cover the times. Look at the clocks and say the times.

c 🔊 5.24 Listen and draw the times on the clocks.

> 🔍 **The time**
> 1 You can also say the time with numbers, e.g., 7:15 = (a) quarter after seven **OR** seven fifteen.
> 2 60 minutes /ˈmɪnəts/ = one hour /ˈaʊər/.
>
> 🔍 **American and British English**
> (nine)-thirty = American English
> half past (nine) = British English

d Practice with a partner.

Number 1. What time is it?   *It's twenty to nine.*

e 🅖 **Communication** What time is it? **A** p.79 **B** p.83 Ask and answer about times.

3 PRONUNCIATION /ɑ/, silent consonants

a ◀ 5.25 Listen and repeat the words and sound.

clock	what Oxford sorry coffee

b ◀ 5.26 Listen and repeat the words. Practice saying them.

eight half hour know listen two Wednesday
what write

> 🔍 **Silent letters**
> Some English words have a "silent letter," e.g., in *where*, you don't pronounce the *h* /wɛr/.

c ◀ 5.27 Listen to the conversations. Then practice with a partner.

A What time is it?
B It's eight-thirty.

A Is the meeting on Wednesday?
B I don't know.

A Listen and write the answer. What's half of four?
B That's easy! Two!

4 VOCABULARY saying how you feel

a ◀ 5.28 Listen and repeat the sentences.

1 I'm tired.   2 I'm cold.   3 I'm <u>hun</u>gry.

4 I'm hot.   5 I'm <u>thir</u>sty.

b Match the sentences in **a** to a–e.

a ⬜ Time for lunch.
b ⬜ Time for bed.
c ⬜ It's 41° (degrees /dɪˈɡriz/) this morning.
d ⬜ I need a glass of water.
e ⬜ It's 95°!

c ◀ 5.29 Listen and check. How do <u>you</u> feel right now?

5 ▶ A NIGHT OUT

a ◀ 5.30 Watch or listen to Jenny and Amy. Check (✓) the two places they go to.

⬜ a store
⬜ a café
⬜ a theater
⬜ a club
⬜ a restaurant

b Watch or listen again. Complete sentences 1–3 with times.

1 The show is at _____.
2 Jenny and Amy meet at _____.
3 The show ends at _____.

6 USEFUL PHRASES

◀ 5.31 Listen and repeat the useful phrases.

I need to go.	What a great show!
You need to hurry.	It's late and I'm tired.
You're an hour late.	Come on.
I'm really sorry.	OK. Let's go.
Don't worry.	

🔵 **Go online** to watch the video and review the lesson

6A A school reunion

> What does she do?
>
> She's a journalist. She works for a newspaper.

1 VOCABULARY jobs and places of work

a Look at the photos. What are their jobs?

1 He's a **t**_____ **dr**_____.
2 She's a **t**_____.
3 He's a **r**_____.

b **V** p.124 **Vocabulary Bank** Jobs and places of work

c Choose a job from **Vocabulary Bank** Jobs and places of work. Ask five other students the questions. Answer their questions.

(What do you do?   (Where do you work?

2 GRAMMAR simple present: *he, she, it*

a Look at the picture. Why are the people together?

b 🔊 6.4 Cover the conversation and listen. Mark the sentences **T** (true) or **F** (false).

1 Anna is a journalist.
2 She works for a magazine.
3 Matt is a teacher.
4 He teaches English.
5 Laura is Matt's daughter.

c Listen again and read the conversation. Check your answers.

d Read the conversation again and complete the chart.

simple present, third person	
I / you	*he / she*
➕ **I work** for a newspaper.	**She** _____ for a newspaper.
➖ **I don't wear** glasses.	**She** _____ glasses.
❓ What **do you** do?	What _____ **he** do?

e **G** p.102 **Grammar Bank 6A**

Julia	Who's that over there?
Sarah	It's Anna, you know, the intelligent girl.
Julia	She's very different! Her hair's blonde.
Sarah	Yes, and she doesn't wear glasses now.
Julia	What does she do?
Sarah	She's a journalist. She works for a newspaper – *The Times*, I think.
Julia	Is she good?
Sarah	I don't know. I don't read *The Times*.

Julia	And who's that man with gray hair? Is it Matt?
Sarah	Yes!
Julia	What does he do?
Sarah	He's a teacher. He teaches Spanish.
Julia	Where does he work?
Sarah	At our old school!
Julia	No! At our old school?
Sarah	Yes, and he's married to Laura!
Julia	Laura? From our class? Is she here?
Sarah	Yes, she's with Matt.
Julia	Very nice shoes.
Sarah	I know, right? They're amazing!

Laura	Sarah, Julia, hi! Great to see you!
Julia	Hi, Laura. Wow, I *love* your shoes – they're beautiful…

3 PRONUNCIATION third person -es

a ◐ 6.6 Listen and ⟨circle⟩ the words where final -es = /ɪz/.

does finishes goes likes lives teaches watches writes

b ◐ 6.7 Listen. Change the sentences. Use the third person.

1 ⟩) *I live in New York. He...* (*He lives in New York.*

4 READING

a In what jobs in <u>your</u> country do people need to speak English?

b Read the article. Complete 1 and 2 with a job from **Vocabulary Bank** Jobs and places of work **p.124.**

Do you speak **English** at work?

What do these people have in common: A banker in Mexico City, a taxi driver in Ankara, and a worker in the Hitachi electronics factory in Tokyo? They all speak English at work. Do you speak English at work? Write and tell us.

1 Antonio I work in a restaurant in Lima. I'm a _____. I speak English at work every day because a lot of tourists come here. I help customers with the menu and I say what the special dishes are. They are very happy because they can talk to me in English. A lot of tourists don't speak Spanish, but they usually speak English.

2 Charlotte I'm a _____ and I work in an office in Buenos Aires. It's a multinational company. When people from other countries visit the company, I need to welcome them in English. I also need to answer the phone in English. When we have meetings, we all speak in English because it's the language of the company.

c ◐ 6.8 Now read again and listen. Check your answers.

d Answer the questions with a partner.

1 Why does Antonio speak English at work?
2 How does he help people?
3 Who does Charlotte work for?
4 What two things does she do in English?
5 Why do they speak English in meetings in her company?

> 🔎 *Why...? Because...*
> We use *Why...?* /waɪ/ to ask for a reason, and *Because...* /bɪˈkʌz/ to give a reason.
> **Why** are the tourists happy? **Because** they can talk to Antonio in English.

5 PRONUNCIATION & SPEAKING sentence rhythm

a ◐ 6.9 Listen to the conversation.

A **What** does he **do**?
B He's a **nurse**.
A **Where** does he **work**?
B He **works** in a <u>hospital</u>.
A Does he **speak** <u>Eng</u>lish at **work**?
B **No**, he <u>doesn't</u>.
A Does he **like** his **job**?
B **Yes**, he **does**.

b ◐ 6.10 Listen again and repeat. <u>Copy</u> the <u>rhythm</u>.

c Think of two people you know who have jobs. Ask and answer with a partner.

What / he (she) do?
Where / he (she) work?
/ he (she) speak English at work?
/ he (she) like his (her) job? Why?

Person number one is my mother.)

(*What does she do?*

6 WRITING

Write paragraphs about the two people in **5c.**

My mother is a teacher. She works
at an elementary school in São Paulo. She
doesn't speak English at work. She loves
her job because she likes children!

WORDS AND PHRASES TO LEARN 6A

p.131 Listen and repeat the words and phrases.

Go online to review the lesson

| What time do you usually get up? | I get up at 7:00. |

G adverbs of frequency   **V** a typical day   **P** /y/ and /yu/, sentence rhythm

1 LISTENING & SPEAKING

a Read the questions in **Are you a morning person?** and think about your answers.

b 🔊6.12 Look at the photos and listen to Hannah answer the questions in **a**. Does she like mornings?

Hannah is a concert planner. Her son, Kit, is three years old.

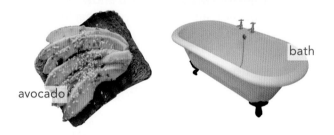

avocado   bath

c Listen again and write her answers to questions 1–8.

d 🔊6.13 Listen and repeat questions 1–8.

e Ask your partner the questions. Is he or she a "morning person"? Why (not)?

2 VOCABULARY a typical day

a **V** p.125 **Vocabulary Bank** A typical day

b Can you remember? Mime or draw five verb phrases for your partner to guess.

Are you a *morning* person?

1. What time do you usually get up?

2. Do you usually feel tired?

3. Do you take a shower or a bath in the morning?

4. Do you always have breakfast? Where?

5. What do you have for breakfast?

6. What time do you go to work (school)?

7. Do you usually need to hurry in the morning?

8. Do you like mornings? Why (not)?

3 GRAMMAR adverbs of frequency

a Match sentences 1–4 to a–d.

	M	Tu	W	Th	F
1 I always get up at 8:00, … c	✓	✓	✓	✓	✓
2 I never drink coffee, …	✗	✗	✗	✗	✗
3 I usually finish work at 6:00, …	✓	✓	✓	✓	✗
4 I sometimes watch TV, …	✗	✓	✗	✗	✓

a but on Fridays I finish at 3:00.
b or I read and listen to music.
c because I start work at 9:00.
d because I don't like it.

b **G** p.102 **Grammar Bank 6B**

4 PRONUNCIATION /y/ and /yu/, sentence rhythm

a 🔊 6.17 Listen and repeat the words and sounds.

Ÿ yacht	yes you young yellow
/yu/	usually university uniform beautiful

b 🔊 6.18 Listen and repeat. <u>C</u>opy the <u>rhy</u>thm.

What time do you **usually have lunch?**
At **one-<u>thir</u>ty**.
What time do you **usually have <u>din</u>ner?**
At about **eight** o'<u>clock</u>.
What time do you **usually go** to **bed?**
At **e<u>le</u>ven-<u>thir</u>ty**.

c Ask and answer the questions with a partner.

d In pairs, make true sentences about <u>you</u>. Use *always, usually, sometimes,* or *never.*

- listen to the radio in the car
- read a newspaper in the morning
- speak English outside class
- watch TV in the evening
- have a big lunch
- do housework on the weekend
- eat fast food
- drink espresso

> *I always listen to the radio in the car. I listen to pop music.*

5 SPEAKING & WRITING

a Use the pictures in **Vocabulary Bank** A typical day **p.125** to tell your partner about your typical evening. Use adverbs of frequency.

> *I never make dinner. My father makes it. We usually have dinner at eight-thirty.*

b Write about <u>your</u> typical morning and afternoon. Use adverbs of frequency (*always, usually,* etc.) and time words (*then, after breakfast,* etc.).

6 ▶ VIDEO LISTENING A day in the life of a New York tour guide

a Look at photos A–F from the video *A day in the life of a New York tour guide.* With a partner, number the photos 1–6.

b Watch the video and check your order.

c Watch again. Mark the sentences **T** (true) or **F** (false).
1 Peter lives in an apartment in Brooklyn.
2 He gets up at seven o'clock.
3 He usually has an omelet for breakfast.
4 He works for a company called Real World Tours.
5 His tours begin at eleven o'clock.
6 He usually has a sandwich for lunch.
7 The tour ends on Wall Street.
8 Peter goes home by subway.
9 In the evening he reads or watches TV.
10 Every day he walks about ten miles.

d Watch some extracts from the video. Complete the sentences with a "time" word or phrase.
1 _____ _____ he goes there by subway.
2 _____ work, Peter takes the subway back to Brooklyn.
3 _____ he relaxes.

e Do you think Peter's job is easy or difficult? Why?

WORDS AND PHRASES TO LEARN 6B

p.131 Listen and repeat the words and phrases.

Go online to watch the video and review the lesson

GRAMMAR

Circle a or b.

_____'s your name?
a Who   b **What**

1 In Japan, we _____ rice for breakfast.
a have   b has

2 They _____ meat.
a don't eat   b not eat

3 You _____ a lot of fast food. It isn't good for you.
a eats   b eat

4 I _____ tea. I prefer coffee.
a don't drink   b 'm not drink

5 _____ you want a hot chocolate?
a Are   b Do

6 A Do they live near here?
B Yes, they _____.
a do   b live

7 _____ Mexican food?
a Like you   b Do you like

8 A What time _____?
B At 5:30.
a do we arrive   b we arrive

9 _____ she speak Spanish?
a Do   b Does

10 He _____ for a fashion magazine.
a works   b work

11 My brother _____ children.
a don't have   b doesn't have

12 She _____ to the gym after work.
a gos   b goes

13 He _____ a shower before breakfast.
a always takes   b takes always

14 I _____ to bed before 12:00.
a don't never go   b never go

15 What time _____ lunch?
a you have usually   b do you usually have

VOCABULARY

a Write the words.

bread   1 _____   2 _____

3 _____   4 _____   5 _____

b Complete the verbs.

t_ake_ a shower

1 **r**_____ the newspaper
2 **l**_____ to the radio
3 **g**_____ shopping
4 **l**_____ in an apartment
5 **g**_____ up in the morning

6 **w**_____ TV
7 **d**_____ housework
8 **sp**_____ English
9 **h**_____ two children
10 **dr**_____ tea

c Complete the words.

My wife's a **t**_eacher_ in a school in the city.
1 I don't have a job. I'm **u**_____.
2 He's a **w**_____. He works in a restaurant.
3 My grandfather doesn't work now. He's **r**_____.
4 My sister's a **n**_____. She works in a big hospital.
5 He's a **j**_____. He writes for the _New York Times_.

d Write the times.

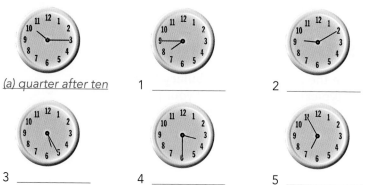

(a) quarter after ten   1 _____   2 _____

3 _____   4 _____   5 _____

PRONUNCIATION

a Write the words for the sound pictures.

🚲 *bike*	3	🐦
1 ⛵	4	🌼
2 🦘	5	🧒

b 🅿 p.134–5 **Sound Bank** Look at more words with the sounds in **a**, and these sounds:

🦜 🦬

Practice saying the example words.

c Underline the stressed syllable.

<u>break</u>|fast   2 po|lice|man   4 u|su|a|lly
1 po|ta|toes   3 al|ways   5 cer|e|al

CAN YOU understand this text?

a Read the text and complete it with words from the list.

coffee   diet   don't   every   good   hamburgers   meat
potatoes   small   stop   vegetables

EAT THE JAPANESE WAY

Doctors say that the traditional <u>diet</u> in Japan and other Asian countries is very healthy.

WHY IS IT GOOD FOR YOU?

In Japan, people don't eat a lot of red ¹_____, butter, or cheese. They eat a lot of rice and fish and fresh fruit and ²_____. This diet is very ³_____ for your heart and people in Japan live longer than in other countries.

HOW TO EAT LIKE THE JAPANESE

◆ Eat rice with your meals and don't eat a lot of ⁴_____, especially French fries.
◆ Eat a lot of fish. ⁵_____ eat a lot of meat, for example, steak and ⁶_____.
◆ Eat fresh fruit and vegetables ⁷_____ day.
◆ Drink green tea, not ⁸_____.
◆ Eat on ⁹_____ plates. Eat slowly. ¹⁰_____ eating when you are full.

b Do <u>you</u> eat "the Japanese way"?

▶ CAN YOU understand these people?

◀)) 6.20 **Watch or listen and answer the questions.**

| 1 John | 2 Josh | 3 Lisa | 4 Susan | 5 Shrenik |

1 For breakfast John usually has ____.
  a tea and cereal
  b tea and toast
  c coffee and toast
2 Josh lives in ____.
  a a house in Chinatown
  b a house near Chinatown
  c an apartment in Chinatown
3 Lisa's son is ____.
  a 1
  b 6
  c 16
4 Susan ____.
  a doesn't work
  b is a taxi driver
  c works in an office
5 Shrenik gets up at ____ during the week.
  a 5:50 a.m.
  b 6:50 a.m.
  c 7:50 a.m.

CAN YOU say this in English?

Check (✓) the boxes.

Can you...?	Yes, I can.
1 say what you do (your job or activity)	☐
2 ask what other people do	☐
3 say what you have for breakfast	☐
4 say what people eat in your country	☐
5 ask and say what time it is	☐
6 say what you do on a typical day	☐
7 ask about other people's days	☐

Communication

1B WHERE IS IT? Student A

a Ask **B** questions for your cities.

(*Where's Izmir?*

1 **Izmir** is in Turkey.
2 **Atlanta** is in the United States.
3 **Hanoi** is in Vietnam.
4 **Curitiba** is in Brazil.
5 **Cusco** is in Peru.
6 **Montreal** is in Canada.
7 **Hong Kong** is in China.
8 **Salta** is in Argentina.

b Answer **B**'s questions with a country.

(*It's in...* (*I think it's in...* (*I don't know.*   ← p.8

PE1 HIT THE SHIPS Student A

a Draw five "ships" in **Your ships**.

Your ships

	1	2	3	4	5	6	7	8	9	10
A										
B										
C										
D										
E										
F										
G										
H										
I										
J										

One ship = three squares

B's ships

	1	2	3	4	5	6	7	8	9	10
A										
B										
C										
D										
E										
F										
G										
H										
I										
J										

b Try to "hit" **B**'s ships. Say a square, e.g., *H8*. If **B** says *Hit*, check (✓) the square in **B**'s ships. If **B** says *Nothing*, cross out (✗) the square.

H8?) (*Nothing.*   *B7?*) (*Hit!*

c **B** says a square. Say *Hit* or *Nothing*.   ← p.10

2A IS SUSHI CHINESE? Student A

_____ sushi Chinese?

Gisele Bündchen is Brazilian.

_____ the Rolling Stones American?

Hyundai cars are Korean.

_____ Mount Fuji Japanese?

Tacos are Mexican.

_____ Victoria Beckham Canadian?

Antonio Banderas is Spanish.

_____ Machu Picchu Peruvian?

Coke and Pepsi are American.

a Ask **B** about 1–5. Use *Is...?* or *Are...?* Check (✓) if the answer is yes. If the answer is no, write the nationality.

(*Is sushi Chinese?*

b Answer **B**'s question about 6–10.

No, he / she / it isn't. He / She / It's...)
Yes, they are.)
No, they aren't. They're...)   ← p.13

2B PERSONAL INFORMATION Student A

a Interview **B** and complete **B**'s form.

What's your first name?) (*Chris.*
How do you spell it?) (*C-H-R-I-S.*

Student B

First name	
Last name	
Nationality	
Address	
Zip code	
Age	
Married ☐ Single ☐	
Phone number	home
	cell
Email address	

b Answer **B**'s questions. Use the information in the **YOU** form.

YOU

First name	Alex
Last name	Barrett
Nationality	American
Address	15 Hill Drive, Los Angeles, CA
Zip code	90041
Age	25
Married ☐ Single ✓	
Phone number	home 323-555-0679
	cell 323-555-4198
Email address	abarrett65@mymail.com

← p.15

3B HOW MUCH ARE THESE WATCHES? Student A

a Look at your picture. You are a customer. Ask **B** about the missing prices. Use *this / that* for singular objects **OR** *these / those* for plural objects. Write the prices.

How much is this mug?) (*It's...*

b Now **B** is a customer. Answer **B**'s questions with a price.

(*It's / They're...dollars.*

← p.21

PE3 WHAT TIME IS IT? Student A

a Ask **B** a question to complete the time on clock 1.

(*Clock 1: What time is it?*

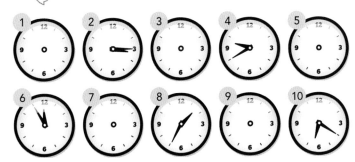

b Answer **B**'s question about clock 2.

(*It's...*

c Continue with the other clocks.   ← p.34

3A MEMORY GAME Students A+B

a   Look at the photo for 30 seconds.

b   Close your book. In pairs, can you remember all the things?   *A watch.*) (*No, two watches, I think.*   ⟵ p.18

1B WHERE IS IT? Student B

a Answer **A**'s questions with a country.

(It's in... (I think it's in... (I don't know.

b Ask **A** questions for your cities.

(Where's Acapulco?

1 **Acapulco** is in Mexico.
2 **Las Vegas** is in the United States.
3 **Manchester** is in England.
4 **Busan** is in Korea.
5 **Osaka** is in Japan.
6 **Santiago** is in Chile.
7 **Riyadh** is in Saudi Arabia.
8 **Valencia** is in Spain.

⬅ p.8

PE1 HIT THE SHIPS Student B

a Draw five "ships" in **Your ships**.

Your ships

	1	2	3	4	5	6	7	8	9	10
A										
B										
C										
D										
E										
F										
G										
H										
I										
J										

One ship
= three
squares

A's ships

	1	2	3	4	5	6	7	8	9	10
A										
B										
C										
D										
E										
F										
G										
H										
I										
J										

b **A** says a square, e.g., *H8*. If you have a ship in H8, say *Hit*. If not, say *Nothing*.

H8?) (Nothing.   B7?) (Hit!

c Try to "hit" **A**'s ships. Say a square, e.g., *B3*. If **A** says *Hit*, check (✓) the square in **A**'s ships. If **A** says *Nothing*, cross out (✗) the square.

⬅ p.10

2A IS SUSHI CHINESE? Student B

Sushi is Japanese.

_____ Gisele Bündchen English?

The Rolling Stones are British.

_____ Hyundai cars Vietnamese?

Mount Fuji is Japanese.

_____ tacos Mexican?

Victoria Beckham is British.

_____ Antonio Banderas Chilean?

Machu Picchu is Peruvian.

_____ Coke and Pepsi British?

a Answer **A**'s question about 1–5.

Yes, he / she / it is.)
No, he / she / it isn't. He / She / It's...)
Yes, they are.)
No, they aren't. They're...)

b Ask **A** about 6–10. Use *Is...?* or *Are...?* Check (✓) if the answer is yes. If the answer is no, write the nationality.

(Is Gisele Bündchen English?

⬅ p.13

2B PERSONAL INFORMATION Student B

a Answer **A**'s questions. Use the information in the **YOU** form.

YOU	
First name	Chris
Last name	Lennox
Nationality	American
Address	81 West Street, Bridgeport, CT
Zip code	06605
Age	31
Married ✓ Single ☐	
Phone number	home 203-555-8124
	cell 203-555-0997
Email address	chris71@mac.com

b Interview **A** and complete **A**'s form.

What's your first name?) (*Chris.*
How do you spell it?) (*C-H-R-I-S.*

Student A	
First name	
Last name	
Nationality	
Address	
Zip code	
Age	
Married ☐ Single ☐	
Phone number	home
	cell
Email address	

← p.15

3B HOW MUCH ARE THESE WATCHES? Student B

a Look at your picture. **A** is a customer. Answer **A**'s questions with a price.

(*It's / They're...dollars.*

b Now you are a customer. Ask **A** about the missing prices. Use *this / these* **OR** *that / those*. Write the prices.

How much is this flag?) (*It's...*

← p.21

PE3 WHAT TIME IS IT? Student B

a Answer **A**'s question about clock 1.

(*It's...*

b Ask **A** a question to complete the time on clock 2.

(*Clock 2: What time is it?*

c Continue with the other clocks.   ← p.34

Writing

1 A FORM

a Look at the form. Match each part to a question a–h below.

- a ☐ Are you married?
- b ☐ What's your home phone number?
- c ☐ What's your zip code?
- d ☐ How old are you?
- e ☐ What's your email?
- f ☐ *1* What's your name?
- g ☐ What's your cell phone number?
- h ☐ What's your address?

CREDIT CARD Application form

1 First name
_____

Last name
_____

Title: Mr. ☐   Ms. ☐   Mrs. ☐

2 Age
_____

3 Married ☐   Single ☐
Divorced / Separated ☐

4 Address
_____

5 Zip code
_____

6 Email
_____

Phone number 7 home
_____

8 cell phone
_____

---

b Complete the form for you. Check (✓) your title, too.

> 🔍 **Titles**
> Mr. = a man, Ms. = a woman,
> Mrs. = a married woman
>
> **Capital letters**
> **A**dam **D**avis **NOT** ~~adam davis~~
> 245 **G**reen **S**treet **NOT** ~~245 green street~~
> **L**ondon **NOT** ~~london~~
> **M**iami, **F**lorida **NOT** ~~miami, florida~~

⬅ p.15

2 A POST ABOUT A PHOTO

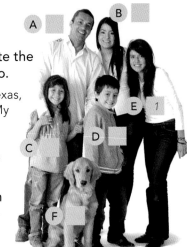

a Read about Ava and her family. Write the numbers of the people on the photo.

My name is [1]Ava and I'm from Dallas, Texas, in the US. This is a photo of my family. My father's name is [2]Ron, and my mother's name is [3]Linda. I have a sister, [4]Ariana, and a brother, [5]Will. We have a dog. His name is [6]Rocky. Do you like my photo?

b Look at the highlighted punctuation in the text and read the information box.

> 🔍 **Punctuation**
> | period (.) | My name is Ava and I'm from Dallas. **NOT** ~~My name is Ava and I'm from Dallas~~ |
> |---|---|
> | comma (,) | I have a sister, Ariana, and a brother, Will. |
> | question mark (?) | Do you like my photo? |
> | apostrophe (') | I'm from Dallas. **NOT** ~~Im from Dallas.~~ My father's name… **NOT** ~~My fathers name…~~ |

c Post a photo of your family and write about it.   ⬅ p.25

3 A COMMENT POST

a Read Marcos's comment. Do you like his breakfast?

> **LET'S CHAT! TODAY'S QUESTION:**
>
> Is breakfast important for you? What do you have? Where do you have it?
>
> **Mark, Los Angeles, US** *7 mins ago*
>
> Breakfast is very important for me! I have fruit, usually an orange or an apple.
> Then I have milk, cereal, and a glass of orange juice.
> I usually have breakfast at home, but on weekends I have it at a café near my house. I think my breakfast is very healthy.
>
>

b Look at the highlighted words. Complete sentences 1–3 with *and*, *or*, or *but*.

1 I eat fish, _____ I don't eat meat.
2 Do you have tea _____ coffee for breakfast?
3 I have a brother _____ a sister.

c Write a comment about <u>your</u> breakfast. What do you have? Is it healthy? Use *and*, *but*, and *or* to connect.   ⬅ p.31

Listening

🔊 **1.42**

Hello. I'm Rob. I'm from London. I'm a journalist. Today I'm in Poland. I'm not on holiday. I'm here for work.

🔊 **1.45**

Hi. I'm Jenny Zielinski. I'm from New York. Tomorrow's my birthday, and my favorite restaurant in New York is Locanda Verde. It's Italian.

🔊 **1.46**

Waiter Locanda Verde. Good morning. How can I help you?
Jenny Hello. A table for tomorrow, please.
Waiter Tomorrow…uh, Tuesday?
Jenny Yes, that's right.
Waiter How many people?
Jenny Three.
Waiter What time?
Jenny Seven o'clock.
Waiter What's your name, please?
Jenny Jenny Zielinski. That's Z-I-E-L-I-N-S-K-I.
Waiter Thank you, Ms., uh, Zielinski. OK. So, a table for three on Tuesday at seven.
Jenny Great. Thanks. Bye.
Waiter Goodbye. See you tomorrow.

🔊 **2.26**

1 **A** Great. OK, see you on Tuesday.
   B Yes. Oh, what's your cell phone number?
   A It's, uh, 303-555-0415.
2 **A** Thank you. What's your address, please?
   B It's 57 Oak Street.
3 **A** Come in…sit down. You're Martin Lee, right?
   B Yes.
   A And how old are you, Mr. Lee?
   B I'm 39…
4 **A** Thank you very much. Uh, one more thing. What's your email?
   B It's james85@geemail.com

🔊 **3.2**

What are the top things people look for every day? At number 8, it's…wallets and change purses.

At number 7, umbrellas.

At number 6, bank cards – credit cards or debit cards.

At number 5, phone chargers.

And now for the top four.

At number 4, glasses and sunglasses.

At number 3, pens and pencils.

And at number 2, cell phones.

And at number 1, – yes, that's right – keys. House keys and car keys.

So, try to find a safe place…

🔊 **3.8**

1 Please take out your laptops… All laptops out, please.
2 Please turn off all cell phones and electronic devices.
3 **A** Excuse me. Is this your bag?
   B Oh yes! Thank you very much!
4 **A** Hi. My name's Sam Smith. I have a reservation.
   B Can I see your passport, please?
   A Sure, here you are.
5 **A** OK, Ms. Jones. You're in room 315. Here's your key.
   B Thank you very much. Uh, where's the elevator?

🔊 **3.13**

Man Excuse me, Miss. Is this your cell phone?
Woman Oh! Yes, it is. Thank you very much.
Man You're welcome. It's a very nice phone! The new iPhone.
Woman Sorry? Oh yes.
Man A souvenir for your family? A T-shirt is only $25!
Woman OK. A Yankees T-shirt, please.
Man And a mug?
Woman Yes, and a mug!

🔊 **3.20**

1 **Man** *The New York Times*, please.
   Woman Here you are.
   Man How much is it?
   Woman It's two dollars and fifty cents.
2 **Man** An umbrella, please.
   Woman For how much?
   Man Fifteen euros, please.
   Woman Here you are.
   Man Thanks.
3 **Man 1** A memory card, please.
   Man 2 Two gigs or four?
   Man 1 Two, please. How much is it?
   Man 2 Nine dollars and forty-nine cents.
   Man 1 Is a credit card OK?
   Man 2 Sure.
4 **Woman** A one-way ticket to Oxford, please.
   Man Thirty pounds twenty p, please.
   Woman Here you are.
   Man Thank you.

🔊 **3.25**

Assistant Hi. How can I help you?
Jenny Hi. How much is this tuna salad?
Assistant It's seven twenty.
Jenny OK, fine. And this mineral water, please.
Assistant That's nine dollars seventy cents.
Jenny Here you are.
Assistant Thank you. Have a nice day.
Amy Jenny!
Jenny Amy! Hi, how are you?
Amy I'm fine. How are you?
Jenny I'm fine, too.
Amy What's that?
Jenny Oh, just a salad and some water.
Amy You are good! Look, wait for me. We can have lunch together in the park.
Jenny Sure! Great idea.
Amy Can I have a cheese sandwich, a cappuccino, and a brownie, please?

🔊 4.11

Marina What a nice card!

Carly Yeah, it's from my family.

M Can I see?

C Sure.

M Who's Paul? Is he your brother?

C Yes, he's my brother and Hayley's his girlfriend.

M How old is Paul?

C He's twenty-nine. No, he's thirty.

M What about Shira? Is she your sister?

C No, Shira's my brother Jerry's wife. And Mia's their daughter.

M Oh yeah, I remember. The baby in the photo on your phone.

C Yes. She's so beautiful.

M So who's Nicole?

C She's my sister.

M Is John her husband?

C No, he's her boyfriend – they aren't married. Maybe one day.

M And how old's Nicole?

C She's twenty-six.

M And who's Buddy?

C He's my dog!

M Oh! What kind of dog is he?

🔊 4.13

1 It's a Chevrolet. It's American.

2 It's a Jaguar. It's British.

3 It's a Hyundai. It's Korean.

4 It's a Geely. It's Chinese.

5 It's a SEAT. It's Spanish.

6 It's a Honda. It's Japanese.

🔊 5.6

Anna My favorite meal of the day is dinner. I usually have dinner at home, but sometimes I have dinner a restaurant. I usually have meat or fish and vegetables, and if I'm at a restaurant, I have a cup of coffee.

🔊 5.7

Will My favorite meal of the day is lunch. I'm always hungry then. I have lunch at work. We have a cafeteria there. I have different things for lunch but always with French fries. I love French fries. Sometimes a burger and French fries, sometimes fish and French fries. I drink water with my lunch, but after lunch I have a coffee, an espresso.

Sarah My favorite meal of the day is breakfast. I usually have it at home, but on Wednesdays I have my yoga class and I have breakfast at a café near the yoga studio. At home I have fruit and an egg, and coffee or tea. But at the café I have a muffin and hot chocolate.

🔊 5.15

Taxi driver Where to ma'am?

Eve Hello. To the airport, please.

Taxi driver JFK or Newark?

Eve JFK, please.

Eve Oh dear. The traffic is bad this morning.

Taxi driver Yes. It's terrible. Where are you from?

Eve I'm from Manchester but I live in London. Are you from New York?

Taxi driver No, ma'am, I'm from Puerto Rico.

Eve Oh, do you like New York?

Taxi driver It's a great city, but it's very expensive.

Eve London is very expensive, too. Do you have children?

Taxi driver I have two daughters.

Eve Oh really? I have two sons and a daughter. David and Andrew are in college, and Carla's in high school…

Taxi driver OK. Here we are.

Eve How much is that?

Taxi driver That's $87.50.

Eve Oh. Here's $100. Keep the change.

Taxi driver Thanks. Have a good flight!

Eve I need to hurry. I'm late!

Announcement This is the final call for flight BA641 to London Heathrow. All passengers please proceed to gate B5.

🔊 5.30

Amy Hi. Sorry I'm late. What time's the show?

Jenny Don't worry. It's at eight o'clock.

Amy What time is it now?

Jenny It's OK. It's only twenty to eight.

Amy What a great show!

Jenny Yes, fantastic. I'm hungry. Do you want a pizza?

Amy What time is it?

Jenny Um, quarter to eleven.

Amy It's late and I'm tired.

Jenny Come on. I know a really good Italian restaurant near here.

Amy Oh, OK. Let's go.

🔊 6.12

I Hannah is a concert planner. She has a son, Kit, who's three years old.

I Hannah, what time do you usually get up?

H I get up at 7:00. But I also get up in the night because Kit usually calls me. I tell him to sleep, but he usually comes into my bed.

I Do you usually feel tired?

H Yes, I always feel tired!

I Do you take a shower or a bath in the morning?

H I turn on the TV for Kit and then I take a bath in five minutes.

I Do you always have breakfast?

H Yes, I need breakfast every day!

I Where do you have it?

H I have it in a café on the way to work.

I What do you have for breakfast?

H I have a coffee and sometimes I have some toast with avocado. It's delicious.

I What time do you go to work?

H The perfect time to leave the house is at 8:00, but we usually leave at twenty after eight.

I Do you usually need to hurry in the morning?

H Yes, always!

I Do you like mornings?

H Yes. I love mornings.

I Why?

H Because I love my job, and I'm happy to go to work!

 Go online to listen to the audio and see all the Listening scripts

1A verb *be* (singular): *I* and *you*

🔊 **1.4** Listen and repeat the examples. Then read the rules.

	Full form	Contraction
+	I am Helen. You are Tom.	I'm Helen. You're Tom.
−	I am not Ellen. You are not Dom.	I'm not Ellen. You aren't Dom.

- *I'm Helen.* **NOT** ~~i'm Helen.~~
- *I'm Helen.* **NOT** ~~Am Helen.~~

> 🔍 **Negative contractions**
> *I am not = I'm not*
> *You are not = You aren't* **OR** *You're not*

🔊 **1.5** Listen and repeat the examples. Then read the rules.

?	+	−
Am I in room 2?	Yes, you are.	No, you aren't.
Are you Mike?	Yes, I am.	No, I'm not.

> 🔍 **Word order in questions**
> + *I'm in room 2.*   *You're Tom.*
> ? *Am I in room 2?*   *Are you Tom?*

1B verb *be* (singular): *he, she, it*

🔊 **1.22** Listen and repeat the examples. Then read the rules.

	Full form	Contraction
+	I am from the US. You are from Peru. He is from Brazil. She is from Spain. It is from China.	I'm from the US. You're from Peru. He's from Brazil. She's from Spain. It's from China.

- he = man   she = woman   it = thing

🔊 **1.23** Listen and repeat the examples. Then read the rules.

	Full form	Contraction
+	I am not from Canada. You are not from Vietnam. He is not from Korea. She is not from Japan. It is not from Mexico.	I'm not from Canada. You aren't from Vietnam. He isn't from Korea. She isn't from Japan. It isn't from Mexico.

> 🔍 **Negative contractions**
> *He is not = He isn't* **OR** *He's not*

🔊 **1.24** Listen and repeat the examples. Then read the rules.

?	+	−
Am I in room 2?	Yes, you are.	No, you aren't.
Are you from England?	Yes, I am.	No, I'm not.
Is he from Chile?	Yes, he is.	No, he isn't.
Is she from Turkey?	Yes, she is.	No, she isn't.
Is it good?	Yes, it is.	No, it isn't.

> 🔍 **Word order in questions**
> + *She's from Argentina.*
> ? *Is she from Argentina?*
> ? With *What* and *Where*:
> *What's your name? Where are you from?*
> *Where's he from?*

1A

a Complete with *I'm* or *You're*.

Hello. *I'm* Maria. What's your name?

1 Hi. _____ Tony.

2 Hello. _____ your teacher. _____ in my class.

3 _____ in room 4.

4 _____ in room 3.

b Complete with *I'm not* or *You aren't*.

I'm not Tom. I'm Tony.

1 _____ in room 5. You're in room 4.

2 _____ in room 6. You're in room 7.

3 _____ Marina. I'm Marisa.

c Make questions.

You're Sam.   *Are you Sam*?
1 I'm in room 4.   _____?
2 You're Silvia.   _____?
3 I'm in room 3.   _____?

d Complete the conversations. Use contractions where possible.

A Hello. *Are* you Liz?   **B** No, I_'m_ not. I'm Maria.
1 **A** _____ I in room 8?   **B** No, you _____. You're in room 6.
2 **A** _____ you in room 4?   **B** No, I _____. I'm in room 5.
3 **A** _____ you Henry?   **B** Yes, I _____. Nice to meet you!
4 **A** _____ I in your class?   **B** Yes, you _____. I _____ your teacher.

◀ p.6

1B

a Complete with *He's*, *She's*, or *It's*.

A Where's London?
B *It's* in England.
1 **A** Where's Lisa from?
   B _____ from Canada.
2 **A** Where's Ankara?
   B _____ in Turkey.
3 **A** Where's Mario from?
   B _____ from Brazil.
4 **A** Where's Beijing?
   B _____ in China.
5 **A** Where's Charles from?
   B _____ from England.
6 **A** Where's Maria from?
   B _____ from Peru.
7 **A** Where's Toronto?
   B _____ in Canada.
8 **A** Where's Carlos from?
   B _____ from Mexico.

b Complete with *is*, *'s*, or *isn't*.

A *Is* Ana from Mexico?   **B** No, she *isn't*. She *'s* from Spain.
1 **A** Where _____ Osaka? _____ it in Japan?
   B Yes, it _____.
2 **A** _____ Mark from the US?
   B No, he _____ from Canada.
3 **A** Where _____ she from?   **B** She _____ from Rio.
4 **A** _____ Robert from Canada?
   B No, he _____. He _____ from England.
5 **A** _____ Lima in Mexico?
   B No, it _____. It _____ in Peru.

c Complete the conversations with the correct form of *be*. Use contractions where possible.

A *Are* you from Turkey?   **B** No, I_'m_ not. I _'m_ from Spain.
1 **A** Where _____ Manchester? _____ it in the UK?
   B Yes, it _____.
2 **A** Where _____ Alex from? _____ he from Mexico?
   B No, he _____. He _____ from the US.
3 **A** Where _____ you from?
   B I _____ from Toronto.
4 **A** What _____ your name?
   B My name _____ Ana. I _____ from Chicago.
   A You _____ from Chicago! I _____ from Chicago, too! It _____ a great city.

◀ p.8

Go online to review the grammar for each lesson

2A verb *be* (plural): *we, you, they*

🔊 **2.6** Listen and repeat the examples. Then read the rules.

	Full form	Contraction
be ➕	I am Korean.	I'm Korean.
	You are Brazilian.	You're Brazilian.
	He is Spanish.	He's Spanish.
	She is Turkish.	She's Turkish.
	It is Japanese.	It's Japanese.
	We are American.	**We're** American.
	You are Chilean.	**You're** Chilean.
	They are Peruvian.	**They're** Peruvian.

• *you* = singular and plural

• *they* = men, women, and things

🔊 **2.7** Listen and repeat the examples. Then read the rules.

	Full form	Contraction
be ➖	I am not Korean.	I'm not Korean.
	You are not Brazilian.	You aren't Brazilian.
	He is not Spanish.	He isn't Spanish.
	She is not Turkish.	She isn't Turkish.
	It is not Japanese.	It isn't Japanese.
	We are not American.	**We aren't** American.
	You are not Chilean.	**You aren't** Chilean.
	They are not Peruvian.	**They aren't** Peruvian.

🔍 **Negative contractions**
We are not = We aren't **OR** *We're not*
You are not = You aren't **OR** *You're not*
They are not = They aren't **OR** *They're not*

🔊 **2.8** Listen and repeat the examples. Then read the rules.

be plural, ❓ and short answers

❓	➕	➖
Am I in room 2?	Yes, you are.	No, you aren't.
Are you Linda?	Yes, I am.	No, I'm not.
Is he Brazilian?	Yes, he is.	No, he isn't.
Is she from Peru?	Yes, she is.	No, she isn't.
Is it good?	Yes, it is.	No, it isn't.
Are we late?	Yes, **you are.**	No, **you aren't.**
Are you from the UK?	Yes, **we are.**	No, **we aren't.**
Are they Mexican?	Yes, **they are.**	No, **they aren't.**

🔍 **Word order in questions**
➕ *They're from Canada.*
❓ *Are they from Canada?*

2B *Wh-* and *How* questions with *be*

🔊 **2.18** Listen and repeat the examples. Then read the rules.

Question word(s)	Verb	Subject	
Who	's	Tom?	He's a friend.
What	's	your email?	johng@gmail.com.
Where	are	you from?	I'm from Toronto, Canada.
When	's	the concert?	It's on Tuesday.
How	are	you?	I'm fine, thanks.
How old	is	she?	She's ten.

🔍 **Word order**
➕ Subject, verb   *They're American.*
❓ Verb, subject   *Are they American?*
❓ Question, verb, subject   **Where** *are they* **from?**

Contractions with question words
We can contract *is* after question words.
What's her name? = What is her name?
Where's he from? = Where is he from?
How's Anna? = How is Anna?
How old's Jan? = How old is Jan?
Don't contract *is* in a question when the last word is a pronoun (*he, she, it,* etc.).
How old is she? **NOT** ~~How old's she?~~
Where is he? **NOT** ~~Where's he?~~

2A

a Change the **bold** word(s) to a pronoun: *you, he, she, it, we, they.*

Luisa and **Pedro** are from Lima.   *They*'re from Lima.
1 **Diana and I** are in room 4.   _____'re in room 4.
2 **The Taj Mahal** is in India.   _____'s in India.
3 Are **Mark and James** in Mexico?   Are _____ in Mexico?
4 Where is **Rosa** from?   Where's _____ from?
5 **Mira and Rita** are Brazilian.   _____'re Brazilian.
6 **Paul** isn't in the hotel.   _____ isn't in the hotel.
7 **You and Sara** are in class 2.   _____'re in class 2.
8 **Jim and I** are from the US.   _____'re from the US.
9 **Honda and Toyota** are Japanese.   _____'re Japanese.

b Make ⊞ or ⊟ sentences, or ?. Use *we, you,* or *they.*

Luisa and I / Brazilian   ⊞ *We're Brazilian.*
You and Henry / teachers   ⊟ *You aren't teachers.*
/ Liz and Tom / in Egypt   ? *Are they in Egypt?*
1 Ana and I / Mexican   ⊟ _____
2 You, Max, and John / in class 4 ⊞ _____
3 / Mike and Peter / English   ? _____
4 / Linda and I / in class 4   ? _____
5 You and Lucy / in class 4   ⊟ _____
6 Lucy and I / on vacation   ⊞ _____

c Complete the conversations. Use contractions where possible.

They *aren't* French. They *'re* Spanish, from Madrid.
1 **A** _____ you from the US?
   B No, we _____ American. We _____ English.
2 **A** _____ they Mexican?
   B Yes, they _____. They _____ from Mexico City.
3 Kareem is from Riyadh. He _____ from Jeddah.
4 Sorry, you _____ in room 20. You're in room 22.
5 **A** _____ your name Maria?
   B No, it _____ Maria. It _____ Marta.
6 **A** _____ we late?
   B Yes, you _____. It _____ 9:30!
7 I _____ Sara Smith. I'm Sara Simpson.
8 They _____ from New York. They're from Texas.
9 **A** Where's Laura from?
   B She _____ from Recife.
   A _____ Recife in Brazil?
   B Yes, it _____.

↩ p.12

2B

a Complete with a question word.

_____
~~How~~ How old What (x2) When
Where (x2) Who (x2)
_____

A *How* are you?
B Fine, thanks. And you?
1 **A** _____'s the concert?
   B On Tuesday at 7:30.
   A _____ is it?
   B Chicago.
2 **A** _____'s your name?
   B Jessica.
3 **A** _____ is she?
   B She's my friend, Julia.
   A _____'s she from?
   B Mexico.
4 **A** _____'s your email?
   B It's jbl098@yoohoo.com.
5 **A** _____'s that?
   B My brother Adrian.
   A _____ is he?
   B He's 25.

b Order the words to make questions.

are how old you?   *How old are you?*
1 she who is?   _____
2 what number your cell phone is?   _____
3 is where room 4?   _____
4 married is Marta?   _____
5 your English class is when?   _____
6 your number is phone 555-0362?   _____
7 is his email what?   _____
8 Pedro how is old?   _____

c Write questions to complete the conversation.

A *What's your name*?   **B** Pedro Guzman.
A ¹_____?   **B** Monterrey.
A ²_____ Monterrey?   **B** It's in Mexico.
A ³_____?   **B** pguzman@gmail.com.
A Thanks. ⁴_____?   **B** 81 8150 9304.
A ⁵_____?   **B** I'm 19.

↩ p.14

Ⓝ **Go online** to review the grammar for each lesson

3

3A singular and plural nouns; *a / an*

🔊 **3.3** Listen and repeat the examples. Then read the rules.

Singular nouns; *a / an*		
What is **it**?	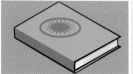 It's **a book**.	It's **a key**.
	 It's **an umbrella**.	It's **an ID card**.

- *What is it?* **NOT** ~~*What's it?*~~
- We use *a / an* + singular noun.
- We use *a* + word beginning with a consonant, e.g., *a bag, a phone.*
- We use *an* + word beginning with a vowel, e.g., *an umbrella.*

🔊 **3.4** Listen and repeat the examples. Then read the rules.

Singular nouns; *a / an*			
	What is it? It's a book.		What are **they**? They're **book**s.
	What is it? It's a key.		What are **they**? They're **key**s.
	What is it? It's a watch.		What are **they**? They're **watch**es.
	What is it? It's a dictionary.		What are **they**? They're **dictionar**ies.

Spelling rules

Singular	Plural	
1 a bag a vacation	bag**s** vacation**s**	add -*s*
2 a class	class**es** /ɪz/	add -*es* (after *ch, sh, s, ss, x*)
3 a country	count**ries**	consonant + *y* = ~~*y*~~ -*ies*

🔍 **the**
Look at **the** board.   Open **the** door.   Close **the** windows.
We use *the* + singular or plural nouns, e.g., *the door, the windows.*

3B *this / that / these / those*

🔊 **3.14** Listen and repeat the examples. Then read the rules.

	What's **this**? It's a key.		What are **these**? They're keys.
	What's **that**? It's a cat.		What are **those**? They're cats.

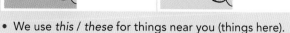

- We use *this / these* for things near you (things here).
- We use *that / those* for things that aren't near you (things there or over there).
- *this / that* = singular, *these / those* = plural.
- We also use *this / that / these / those* for people, e.g., *This is my brother. Who are those girls over there?*

🔍 **this, that, these, those**
This, that, these, and *those* are pronouns or adjectives.
This is my book. (= pronoun)
This book is very nice. (= adjective)

here, there, over there

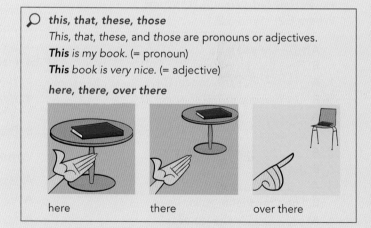

here   there   over there

3A

a Complete the chart.

Singular	Plural
It's a pen.	*They're pens.*
1 _____.	They're phones.
2 It's a watch.	_____.
3 _____.	They're umbrellas.
4 It's a dictionary.	_____.
5 It's a key.	_____.
6 It's a city.	_____.
7 _____.	They're emails.
8 It's a passport.	_____.
9 _____.	They're tablets.

b Write questions and answers.

What is it? *It's a laptop.*

1 _____? _____.

2 _____? _____.

3 _____? _____.

4 _____? _____.

5 _____? _____.

⬅ p.18

3B

a Look at the pictures. Complete the sentences with *this*, *that*, *these*, or *those*.

This isn't a very good book.

1 Are _____ your T-shirts?

2 _____ are my children.

3 **A** Is _____ your cell phone over there?
B No, my cell phone's here.

4 Look at _____! They're great!

5 Who's _____? Is he your brother?

b Look at the pictures. Circle the correct word(s).

Meg What is (this)/ that?
Joe ¹ *They're / It's* a key chain from New York.
Meg Oh, OK.
Joe And ² *these / those* are sunglasses. ³ *It's / They're* great!

Meg Are ⁴ *these / those* mugs?
Joe Yes, ⁵ *it is / they are*. For our coffee. And ⁶ *that / this* is a cap for Joey.
Meg What ⁷ *'s that / are those*?
Joe ⁸ *It's / They're* a T-shirt. It's for you!
Meg Oh...thanks.

⬅ p.21

Go online to review the grammar for each lesson

4A possessive adjectives; possessive 's

▶4.9 Listen and repeat the examples. Then read the rules.

Possessive adjectives	
I'm from the US.	**My** name is Sara.
You're Canadian.	**Your** name is Kim.
He's from China.	**His** name is Ming.
She's Japanese.	**Her** name is Satoko.
It's a Turkish restaurant.	**Its** name is Kebob Kitchen.
We're from Brazil.	**Our** names are Selma and Luis.
You're Chilean.	**Your** names are Matias and Pia.
They're from Mexico.	**Their** names are Pedro and Maria.

- *your names, our books, their coats* **NOT** *yours names, ours books, theirs coats*
- *its* = for things or animals, e.g.,
  Pizzeria Marco is a good restaurant. **Its** *phone number is 212-555-3387.*
  Senegal is in Africa. **Its** *flag is red, yellow, and green.*
  Look at that fish! **Its** *eyes are yellow.*

> 🔍 **It's or its?**
> *It's = it is* **It's** *a Turkish restaurant.*
> *Its = possessive* **Its** *name is Kebob Kitchen.*

▶4.10 Listen and repeat the examples. Then read the rules.

Possessive 's
This is Jack's car.
Ella is Ben's wife.
Maria is Carlos's sister.
My sister's name is Molly.
This is my parents' house.

- We use 's after a person to talk about family and things, e.g., *Ann's brother, Jim's car.*
- We use ' after plural people, e.g., *my brothers' room* (= two brothers).

> 🔍 **'s**
> *She's American. Her name's Emma.* ('s = is)
> *Emma is Maria's daughter.* ('s = possessive s)
>
> **pronunciation of 's**
> *'s usually = /s/, e.g., Jack's or /z/, e.g., Maria's.*
> *'s after a name that ends in s = /ɪz/, e.g., Carlos's = /ˈkɑrlasɪz/.*

4B adjectives

▶4.19 Listen and repeat the examples. Then read the rules.

1 An Audi is **expensive**. It's **fast**.
2 An Audi is an **expensive** car. It's a **fast** car.
3 They're **old houses**. My glasses are **new**.
4 He's **tall**. She's **tall**, too.

1 We use adjectives after the verb *be*, e.g.,
  An Audi is expensive. **NOT** ~~*An Audi expensive is.*~~
2 We use adjectives before a noun, e.g.,
  It's a fast car. **NOT** ~~*It's a car fast.*~~
3 Adjectives are the same for singular and plural:
  It's an old house. They're old houses. **NOT** ~~*They're olds houses.*~~
4 Adjectives are the same for and 👤.

4A

a Complete with *my*, *your* (sing.), *his*, *her*, *its*, *your* (pl.), *our*, or *their*.

I'm American. *My* name is William.
1 They're from Vietnam. _____ names are Bihn and Vu.
2 **A** What's _____ name?
  B I'm Julia. Nice to meet you.
3 He's Chilean. _____ name is Roberto.
4 It's a good hotel, and _____ restaurant is fantastic.
5 They're Mexican. _____ last name is Romero.
6 I know a very good restaurant in Paris. _____ name is Café des Fleurs.
7 _____ name is Tina. She's Brazilian.
8 Lisa and Amy are American, but _____ husbands are British.
9 **A** We're Jane and Mark Kelley. We have a reservation.
  B You're in room 22. This is _____ key.
10 Here are _____ coffees. The cappuccino is for you, the latte is for Tom, and the Americano is for me.
11 I'm Azra, and this is _____ husband, Ahmet.
12 **A** Are those your children?
  B No, they aren't. _____ children are over there.

b Write sentences about Sam's family. Use the names and *'s*.

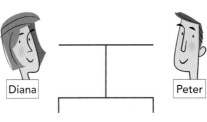

Diana | Peter
Kayla | Sam

Kayla / Sam   *Kayla is Sam's sister.*
1 Peter / Kayla _____
2 Diana / Sam _____
3 Kayla / Peter _____
4 Peter / Diana _____
5 Sam / Peter _____
6 Diana / Peter _____
7 Sam / Kayla _____

← p.24

4B

a Write sentences with *It's a / an* or *They're* + adjective + noun.

 (great)
It's a great restaurant.

 1 (old)
_____

 2 (black)
_____

 3 (new)
_____

 4 (big)
_____

 5 (expensive)
_____

 6 (good)
_____

b Order the words to make sentences.

blue is bag my   *My bag is blue.*
1 beautiful a day it's
_____
2 is husband nice very Amy's
_____
3 questions difficult they're very
_____
4 phone cheap a is this
_____
5 photo it's terrible a
_____
6 Natsuko teacher is fantastic a
_____
7 very is cat old our
_____
8 restaurant this good a very isn't
_____
9 long it's a exercise very
_____
10 is ugly very dog their
_____
11 expensive Japanese movie tickets are very
_____
12 very this is small room a
_____

← p.27

Go online to review the grammar for each lesson

5 GRAMMAR BANK

5A simple present ⊕ and ⊖: *I, you, we, they*

🔊 **5.5** Listen and repeat the examples. Then read the rules.

⊕	⊖
I have cereal for breakfast.	**I don't have** eggs for breakfast. (*don't = do not*)
You have rice for lunch.	**You don't have** pasta for lunch.
We have coffee for breakfast.	**We don't have** tea for breakfast.
They have fish for dinner.	**They don't have** meat for dinner.

- We use the simple present to talk about present habits (= things we usually do), e.g., *I have coffee for breakfast,* and things that are always true, e.g., *In my country, we eat a lot of rice.*
- Simple present ⊕ and ⊖ is the same for *I, you* (singular and plural), *we,* and *they.*
- We make ⊖ sentences with *don't,* e.g., *We don't have coffee.* **NOT** ~~We not have coffee.~~

They have fish for dinner.

5B simple present ⟨?⟩: *I, you, we, they*

🔊 **5.12** Listen and repeat the examples. Then read the rules.

⟨?⟩	⊕	⊖
Do I need a ticket?	Yes, **you do.**	No, **you don't.**
Do you live near here?	Yes, **I do.**	No, **I don't.**
Do we have good seats?	Yes, **we do.**	No, **we don't.**
Do they like children?	Yes, **they do.**	No, **they don't.**

- Simple present ⟨?⟩ is the same for *I, you* (singular and plural), *we,* and *they.*
- We use *do* to make questions: *Do you live here?* **NOT** ~~You live here?~~ **OR** ~~Live you here?~~
- Remember the word order for simple present questions is auxiliary (*do, does*), subject (*I, you, he, she,* etc.), base form (*need, live,* etc.).

Do I need a ticket?

5A

a Write ⊞ or ⊟ sentences.

We (have) 🥪 *We have sandwiches* for lunch.

I (not like) 🐟 *I don't like fish.*

1 I (have) 🥚 _____ for breakfast.

2 We (not drink) ☕ _____ in the evening.

3 They (like) 🍫 _____.

4 You (eat) 🥩 _____.

5 We (eat) 🍚 _____ in the evening.

6 I (not have) 🍬 _____ in my coffee.

7 You (not like) 🧀 _____.

8 The children (eat) 🥦 _____.

b Complete with the **bold** verb. Write one ⊞ sentence and one ⊟ sentence.

like
I'm American, but I *don't like* burgers.
My friends and I *like* fast food, especially pizzas and burgers.

1 have
People in the US _____ a big lunch. They usually have a sandwich.
We always _____ lunch with my family on Sundays.

2 eat
I _____ meat. I'm a vegetarian.
They _____ a lot of fish and rice in Japan.

3 drink
You _____ a lot of coffee! It isn't good for you.
They _____ coffee. They only drink tea.

4 go
We _____ to restaurants. They're very expensive.
I don't have breakfast at home.
I _____ to a café. ⬅ p.31

5B

a Complete with *do* or *don't*.

I *don't* live here. I live near the park.
1 **A** _____ you have children?
  B No, I _____.
2 I _____ like this photo. It's terrible.
3 **A** _____ you want a coffee?
  B No, thanks. I _____ drink coffee.
4 I _____ have brothers and sisters. I'm an only child.
5 **A** _____ you listen to music on the radio?
  B I _____ listen to pop music, but I listen to Classic FM. It's a classical music station.
6 **A** Excuse me, _____ you work here?
  B No, I _____. Sorry.
7 **A** _____ you like American TV shows?
  B No, I _____. I _____ watch TV. I read.
8 **A** _____ you have a big family?
  B Yes, I _____. I have two brothers and three sisters.
9 **A** _____ you speak Spanish?
  B No, I _____. I only speak English.
10 **A** _____ you like Saturdays?
  B Yes, I _____. I _____ work on weekends.

b Order the words to make sentences or questions.

umbrella have do you an? *Do you have an umbrella?*
1 know don't I. _____
2 here you near do live? _____
3 like I soccer don't. _____
4 sandwich want you a do? _____
5 building work in the they tall _____
6 sisters two have I. _____
7 Spanish you speak do? _____
8 don't big need a I car. _____
9 Chinese to classes you do go? _____
10 a don't I watch have. _____
11 to in the music car listen you do? _____
12 work I don't Sundays on _____
⬅ p.32

6A simple present: *he, she, it*

🔊**6.5** Listen and repeat the examples. Then read the rules.

+	−	?	+	−
I work.	I don't work.	Do I work?	Yes, I do.	No, I don't.
You work.	You don't work.	Do you work?	Yes, I do.	No, I don't.
He works.	**He doesn't work.**	**Does he work?**	**Yes, he does.**	**No, he doesn't.**
She works.	**She doesn't work.**	**Does she work?**	**Yes, she does.**	**No, she doesn't.**
It works.	**It doesn't work.**	**Does it work?**	**Yes, it does.**	**No, it doesn't.**
We work.	We don't work.	Do we work?	Yes, we do.	No, we don't.
You work.	You don't work.	Do you work?	Yes, you do.	No, you don't.
They work.	They don't work.	Do they work?	Yes, they do.	No, they don't.

- Simple present ⊞ *he / she / it* = verb + *s*.
- Simple present ⊟ *he / she / it* = *doesn't* + verb (*doesn't* = *does not*).
- Simple present ？ *he / she / it* = *Does* + *he / she / it* + verb. Remember the word order for simple present questions (see **5B** p.100).

Spelling rules 3rd person *s*		
I work in an office. I live in Peru.	He works in an office. He lives in Peru.	+ *s*
I watch CNN. I finish work at 8:00.	She watches CNN. The movie finishes at 8:00.	+ *es* (after *ch, sh, s, ss, x*)
I study history.	He studies history.	consonant + *y* = ~~*y*~~ *-ies*

🔍 ***have, go, do***
These verbs are irregular in the *he / she / it* form of the simple present:
I have *he / she / it* **has** /hæz/
I do *he / she / it* **does** /dʌz/
I go *he / she / it* **goes** /goʊz/

？ with *What* and *Where*
What do you do?
Where does he work?

- Spelling rules for 3rd person *s* are the same as for plural nouns.

6B adverbs of frequency

🔊**6.16** Listen and repeat the examples. Then read the rules.

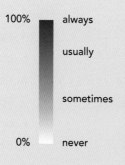

100% — always
usually
sometimes
0% — never

I **always** have breakfast.
They **usually** finish work at 5:00.
She **sometimes** watches TV in the evening.
He **never** eats meat.
Does she **usually** go shopping on Saturday?
What time do you **usually** get up?

- Be careful with the <u>position</u> of adverbs of frequency:
  I always have breakfast. **NOT** ~~Always I have breakfast. I have always breakfast.~~
  Does she usually go shopping on Saturday? **NOT** ~~Does usually she go shopping on Saturday? Usually does she go shopping on Saturday?~~
- With *never*, we use a ⊞ verb: *He never eats meat.* **NOT** ~~He doesn't never eat meat.~~

He never eats meat.

6A

a Rewrite the sentences.

I live in an apartment.   She _lives in an apartment_.

1 They read magazines.
He _____.

2 I study Chinese.
My sister _____.

3 Do you speak English?
_____ he _____?

4 I don't eat fish.
My brother _____.

5 Where do you work?
Where _____ your wife _____?

6 You don't speak Arabic.
Tom _____.

7 Do you like cats?
_____ she _____?

8 I have two brothers.
Andrew _____.

9 What do you eat for lunch?
What _____ he _____?

10 We watch a lot of TV.
My mother _____.

11 What do you do?
What _____ your son _____?

12 We don't need a new car.
Maria _____.

b Put the verb in (parentheses) in the correct form.

They _don't live_ near here. (not live)

1 She _____ to the radio in the car. (listen)

2 My brother _____ to college in Boston. (go)

3 We _____ on weekends. (not work)

4 _____ Angela _____ with her mother? (live)

5 The show _____ at 9:30. (finish)

6 She usually _____ fruit for breakfast. (have)

7 We _____ TV on weekends. (not watch)

8 _____ you _____ tea or coffee? (want)

9 Where _____ your children _____ to school? (go)

10 Linda _____ meat, fish, or eggs. She's a vegan. (not eat)

11 _____ Tran _____ his new job? (like)

12 Luisa _____ brothers or sisters. (not have)

⟵ p.36

6B

a Order the words to complete the sentences.

drink never coffee I
I never drink coffee after dinner.

1 husband goes my sometimes
_____ to the gym.

2 take always I
_____ a shower in the morning.

3 usually we have
_____ breakfast at home.

4 go I never
_____ to bed before 12:00.

5 usually go they do
_____ to work by bus?

6 Jan has sometimes
_____ a sandwich for lunch.

7 close the does restaurant usually
_____ late?

8 goes she never
_____ shopping after work.

9 usually I do
_____ my homework on the weekend.

10 sometimes make I
_____ fish for dinner.

b Complete the sentences in the simple present. Use a verb from the list and the adverb in (parentheses).

do   drink (x2)   eat   finish   get   go
have (x3)   speak   watch

He _never eats_ meat for lunch. (never)

1 Alex _____ _____ to bed very late. (sometimes)

2 We _____ _____ housework on weekends. (always)

3 Do you _____ _____ lunch at home on weekends? (usually)

4 I _____ _____ a bath, I _____ _____ a shower. (never, always)

5 My sister _____ _____ up early. (always)

6 I _____ _____ English at work. (never)

7 We _____ _____ TV after dinner. (sometimes)

8 They _____ _____ coffee in the evening. (never)

9 Does your husband _____ _____ work at 7:30 p.m.? (usually)

10 We _____ _____ tea with milk, but I prefer it with lemon. (sometimes)

⟵ p.38

⊙ **Go online** to review the grammar for each lesson   103

Numbers

1 0–10

a 🔊 1.8 Listen and repeat the numbers.

0 zero /ˈzɪroʊ/
(also "oh" /oʊ/ in phone numbers)
1 one /wʌn/
2 two /tu/
3 three /θri/
4 four /fɔr/
5 five /faɪv/
6 six /sɪks/
7 seven /ˈsɛvn/
8 eight /eɪt/
9 nine /naɪn/
10 ten /tɛn/

> 🔍 **Word stress**
> zero = **ze**ro seven = **se**ven

b Cover the words. Say the numbers.

ACTIVATION Count from 0–10 and from 10–0.

🔙 p.7

2 11–100

11–20

a 🔊 2.21 Listen and repeat the numbers.

11 eleven /ɪˈlɛvn/
12 twelve /twɛlv/
13 thirteen /θərˈtin/
14 fourteen /fɔrˈtin/
15 fifteen /fɪfˈtin/
16 sixteen /sɪksˈtin/
17 seventeen /sɛvnˈtin/
18 eighteen /eɪˈtin/
19 nineteen /naɪnˈtin/
20 twenty /ˈtwɛnti/

21–100

b 🔊 2.22 Listen and repeat the numbers.

21 twenty-one /ˌtwɛnti ˈwʌn/
22 twenty-two /ˌtwɛnti ˈtu/
30 thirty /ˈθərti/
33 thirty-three /θərti ˈθri/
40 forty /ˈfɔrti/
44 forty-four /fɔrti ˈfɔr/
50 fifty /ˈfɪfti/
55 fifty-five /fɪfti ˈfaɪv/
60 sixty /ˈsɪksti/
66 sixty-six /sɪksti ˈsɪks/
70 seventy /ˈsɛvnti/
77 seventy-seven /ˌsɛvnti ˈsɛvn/
80 eighty /ˈeɪti/
88 eighty-eight /eɪti ˈeɪt/
90 ninety /ˈnaɪnti/
99 ninety-nine /naɪnti ˈnaɪn/
100 a / one hundred /ə ˈhʌndrəd/ /wʌn ˈhʌndrəd/

> 🔍 **Word stress – be careful!**
> 30 **thir**ty 13 thir**teen** 40 **for**ty 14 four**teen**, etc.

ACTIVATION Cover the words. Say the numbers.

🔙 p.15

Countries and nationalities

1 COUNTRIES

a 🔊 1.18 Listen and repeat the countries.

1 Argentina /ɑrdʒən'tinə/
2 Brazil /brə'zil/
3 Canada /'kænədə/
4 Chile /'tʃili/
5 China /'tʃaɪnə/
6 England /'ɪŋglənd/
7 Japan /dʒə'pæn/
8 Korea /kə'riə/
9 Mexico /'mɛksɪkoʊ/
10 Peru /pə'ru/
11 Saudi Arabia /'saʊdi ə'reɪbiə/
12 Spain /speɪn/
13 Turkey /'tərki/
14 the United States (the US) /ðə yʊ'naɪtəd steɪts/
15 Vietnam /viɛt'nɑm/

> 🔍 **CAPITAL letters**
> Brazil **NOT** ~~brazil~~.

b Write your country: _____. Practice saying it.

ACTIVATION Cover the words. Look at the photos. Say the countries. ⬅ p.8

2 NATIONALITIES

a 🔊 2.1 Listen and repeat the countries and nationalities.

	Country	Nationality
	Argentina	Argentinian /ɑrdʒən'tɪniən/
	Brazil	Brazilian /brə'zɪlyən/
	Canada	Canadian /kə'neɪdiən/
	Chile	Chilean /tʃɪ'leɪən/
	China	Chinese /tʃaɪ'niz/
	England	English /'ɪŋglɪʃ/
	Japan	Japanese /dʒæpə'niz/
	Korea	Korean /kə'riən/
	Mexico	Mexican /'mɛksɪkən/
	Peru	Peruvian /pə'ruviən/
	Saudi Arabia	Saudi /'saʊdi/
	Spain	Spanish /'spænɪʃ/
	Turkey	Turkish /'tərkɪʃ/
	the United Kingdom	British /'brɪtɪʃ/
	the United States	American /ə'mɛrɪkən/
	Vietnam	Vietnamese /viətnə'miz/

> 🔍 **Word stress**
> For most countries, the word stress is the same on the country and the nationality, e.g., *Brazil, Brazilian*.
> Sometimes it's different:
> Canada → Canadian   China → Chinese
> Japan → Japanese   Vietnam → Vietnamese

b Write your nationality: _____. Practice saying it.

c Read about countries and languages. What's the language in your country?

> 🔍 **Countries and languages**
> The word for a language is sometimes the same as the nationality.
> **England:** nationality *English*, language *English*
> Some are different, e.g.,
> **Canada:** nationality *Canadian*, language *English*
> **Saudi Arabia:** nationality *Saudi*, language *Arabic*

ACTIVATION Cover the words. Look at the flags. Say the countries and nationalities. ⬅ p.12

> 🔵 **Go online** to review the vocabulary for each lesson

The classroom

1 THINGS IN THE CLASSROOM

a 🔊 1.38 Listen and repeat the words.

1 the board /bɔrd/
2 the door /dɔr/
3 a <u>win</u>dow /'wɪndoʊ/
4 a chair /tʃɛr/
5 a coat /koʊt/
6 a table /'teɪbl/
7 a <u>lap</u>top /'læptɑp/
8 a <u>dic</u>tionary /'dɪkʃənɛri/
9 a piece of <u>paper</u> /pis əv 'peɪpər/
10 a pen /pɛn/
11 a bag /bæg/

b Cover the words. Look at the picture. Say the things.

ACTIVATION In pairs, point to things in the classroom. Your partner says the word.

What is it?   (*It's the board.*)
How do you spell it?   (*B-O-A-R-D.*)

2 CLASSROOM LANGUAGE

🔊 1.39 Listen and repeat the phrases.

The teacher says...

1 Look at the board, please.

4 Close your books.

2 <u>O</u>pen your books.

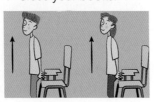
5 Stand up, please.

3 Go to page 10.

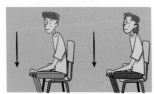
6 Sit down.

You say...

7 How do you spell it?

8 Sorry? Can you re<u>peat</u> that, please?

9 <u>Excuse</u> me. What's *gracias* in <u>E</u>nglish?

10 I don't under<u>stand</u>.

11 I don't know.

12 Sorry I'm late.

ACTIVATION Cover the phrases. Look at the pictures. Say the phrases.

⬅ p.10

Small things

a **◀) 3.1** Listen and repeat the words.

1 a cell phone /sɛl foʊn/
2 a watch /wɑtʃ/
3 a tablet /'tæblət/
4 a wallet /'wɑlət/
   a change purse /tʃeɪndʒ pərs/
5 a pencil /'pɛnsl/
6 a notebook /'noʊtbʊk/
7 glasses /'glæsəz/
8 a photo /'foʊtoʊ/

9 a (phone) charger /'tʃɑrdʒər/
10 an ID card /aɪ 'di kɑrd/
   a passport /'pæspɔrt/
11 an umbrella /ʌm'brɛlə/
12 a camera /'kæmrə/
13 a credit card /'krɛdət kɑrd/
   a debit card /'dɛbət kɑrd/
14 a key /ki/
15 a newspaper /'nuzpeɪpər/

> **a / an**
> **a** bag, **a** key
> **an** ID card, **an** umbrella
>
> **ph**
> ph = /f/, e.g., **ph**one, **ph**oto

b Cover the words. Look at the photo. Say the things.

↩ p.18

People and family

1 PEOPLE

a 🔊 **4.2** Listen and repeat the words.

1 a boy /bɔɪ/
2 a girl /gərl/
3 a man /mæn/
4 a woman /ˈwʊmən/
5 children /ˈtʃɪldrən/
6 friends /frɛndz/

b 🔊 **4.3** Listen and repeat the irregular plurals.

🔍 Irregular plurals	
Singular	**Plural**
a child	children
a man	men
a woman	women
a person	people

ACTIVATION Look at the photos in **a**. Say the words in singular and plural.

(a boy   boys

2 FAMILY

a 🔊 **4.4** Listen and repeat the words.

1 husband /ˈhʌzbənd/
2 wife /waɪf/
3 mother /ˈmʌðər/
4 father /ˈfɑðər/
5 son /sʌn/
6 daughter /ˈdɔtər/
7 brother /ˈbrʌðər/
8 sister /ˈsɪstər/
9 grandmother /ˈgrænmʌðər/
10 grandfather /ˈgrænfɑðər/
11 boyfriend /ˈbɔɪfrɛnd/
12 girlfriend /ˈgərlfrɛnd/

🔍 *parents*
mother + father = parents /ˈpɛrənts/ **NOT** fathers
grandmother + grandfather = grandparents /ˈgrænpɛrənts/

ACTIVATION Cover the words. Look at the photos. Say the family members.
◀ p.24

Adjectives

1 COLORS

🔊 4.16 **Listen and repeat the words.**

black /blæk/

blue /blu/

brown /braʊn/

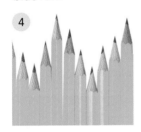
green /grin/

gray /greɪ/

orange /ˈɔrɪndʒ/

pink /pɪŋk/

red /rɛd/

white /waɪt/

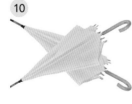
yellow /ˈyɛloʊ/

ACTIVATION Cover the words. Look at the photos. Ask and answer.

What color is it?) (*It's black.*

What color are they?) (*They're blue.*

2 COMMON ADJECTIVES

a 🔊 4.17 Listen and repeat the words.

big /bɪg/   small /smɔl/   old /oʊld/   new /nu/

fast /fæst/   slow /sloʊ/   beautiful /ˈbyutəfl/   ugly /ˈʌgli/

cheap /tʃip/   expensive /ɪkˈspɛnsɪv/   long /lɔŋ/   short /ʃɔrt/

clean /klin/   dirty /ˈdərti/   easy /ˈizi/   difficult /ˈdɪfɪkʌlt/

b Cover the words. Look at the photos. Say the adjectives.

ACTIVATION Test a partner.

What's the opposite of new?) (*Old. What's the opposite of _____?*

d 🔊 4.18 Listen and repeat the positive and negative adjectives.

> 🔍 **Positive and negative adjectives**
> ✓ = good   ✓✓ = very good   ✓✓✓ = great / fantastic
> ✗ = bad   ✗✗ = very bad   ✗✗✗ = awful / terrible
>
> **very**
> You can use **very** before adjectives, e.g., *A Ferrari is **very** expensive. It's a **very** fast car.*

⬅ p.26   **Go online** to review the vocabulary for each lesson

Food and drink

a ◑ **5.2** Listen and repeat the words.

Food

1 fish /fɪʃ/

2 meat /mit/

3 pasta /ˈpɑstə/

4 rice /raɪs/

5 eggs /ɛgz/

6 yogurt /ˈyoʊgərt/

7 vegetables /ˈvɛdʒtəblz/

8 potatoes /pəˈteɪtoʊz/

9 salad /ˈsæləd/

10 fruit /frut/

11 bread /brɛd/

12 butter /ˈbʌtər/

13 cheese /tʃiz/

14 sugar /ˈʃʊgər/

15 a sandwich /ˈsænwɪtʃ/

16 cereal /ˈsɪriəl/

17 chocolate /ˈtʃɑklət/

Drinks

18 coffee /ˈkɔfi/

19 tea /ti/

20 milk /mɪlk/

21 water /ˈwɔtər/

22 orange juice /ˈɔrɪndʒ dʒus/

b ◑ **5.3** Listen and repeat the words and phrases in the box.

ACTIVATION Cover the words in **a**. Look at the photos. Say the words. ⬅ p.30

🔍 **Meals**
breakfast (in the morning)
lunch (in the afternoon)
dinner (in the evening)

Verbs: *have, eat, drink*
I **have** breakfast at 8:00.
I **have** cereal and coffee.
I **eat** a lot of fruit.
I **drink** tea with milk.

eat

drink

Common verb phrases 1

a ◗)5.13 Listen and repeat the phrases.

1 **live** in an apartment
/lɪv ɪn ən əˈpɑrtmənt/

2 **have** breakfast (lunch / dinner)
/hæv ˈbrɛkfəst/ (lʌntʃ / ˈdɪnər)

3 **watch** TV /wɑtʃ ti ˈvi/

4 **listen** to the radio
/ˈlɪsn tə ðə ˈreɪdiəo/

5 **read** the newspaper
/rid ðə ˈnuzpeɪpər/

6 **eat** fast food /it fæst fud/

7 **drink** coffee /drɪŋk ˈkɔfi/

Good morning!

8 **speak** English /spik ˈɪŋglɪʃ/

9 **want** a coffee /wɑnt ə ˈkɑfi/

10 **have** a dog /hæv ə dɔg/

11 **like** cats /laɪk kæts/

12 **work** in a bank /wərk ɪn ə bæŋk/

13 **study** Spanish /ˈstʌdi ˈspænɪʃ/

14 **go** to English classes
/gou tə ˈɪŋglɪʃ ˈklæsɪz/

15 **need** a new car /nid ə nu kɑr/

b ◗)5.14 Cover the phrases. Listen and say the phrase.

1 ◗) *in an apartment* (*live in an apartment*

ACTIVATION Ask and answer with a partner in a different order.

Do you drink coffee?) (*Yes, I do.* (*No, I don't.*

↩ p.33

🔵 **Go online** to review the vocabulary for each lesson

Jobs and places of work

1 WHAT DO THEY DO?

a ◖◗**6.1** Listen and repeat the words.

1 a <u>tea</u>cher /ˈtitʃər/

2 a <u>doc</u>tor /ˈdɑktər/

3 a nurse /nərs/

4 a <u>jour</u>nalist /ˈdʒɜrnəlɪst/

5 a <u>wai</u>ter /ˈweɪtər/
a <u>wai</u>tress /ˈweɪtrəs/

6 a <u>sales</u>person /ˈseɪlzpərsn/

7 a re<u>cep</u>tionist /rɪˈsɛpʃənɪst/

8 a po<u>lice</u>man /pəˈlismən/
a po<u>lice</u>woman /pəˈliswʊmən/

9 a <u>fac</u>tory <u>wor</u>ker /ˈfæktəri ˈwərkər/

10 a <u>ta</u>xi <u>dri</u>ver /ˈtæksi ˈdraɪvər/

b Cover the words. Ask and answer in pairs.

What does she do? *She's a teacher.*
What does he do? *He's a...*

c ◖◗**6.2** Listen and repeat the sentences.

I work for an A<u>mer</u>ican <u>com</u>pany. /ˈkʌmpəni/
I'm in <u>col</u>lege. /ˈkɑlɪdʒ/
I'm a <u>stu</u>dent. /ˈstudnt/
I study eco<u>no</u>mics. /ɛkəˈnɑmɪks/
I'm at school.
I'm unem<u>ployed</u> right now. /ʌnɪmˈplɔɪd/
I'm re<u>tired</u>. /rɪˈtaɪərd/

d What do <u>you</u> do?

I _____.

2 WHERE DO THEY WORK?

a ◖◗**6.3** Listen and repeat the phrases.

1 in a <u>hos</u>pital /ˈhɑspɪtl/

2 in a store /stɔr/

3 in a <u>res</u>taurant /ˈrɛstrənt/

4 in an <u>of</u>fice /ˈɔfəs/

5 in a school /skul/

6 in a <u>fac</u>tory /ˈfæktəri/

7 at home /hoʊm/

8 on the street /strit/

b Cover the phrases. Look at the photos. Say the phrases.

c Ask and answer with a partner.

Where does a doctor work? *In a hospital.*

d Where do <u>you</u> work or study?

I _____.

◖ p.36

A typical day

a 🔊 6.14 Listen and repeat the phrases.

IN THE MORNING

get up /gɛt ʌp/

have breakfast /hæv 'brɛkfəst/

take a shower /teɪk ə 'ʃaʊər/

go to work /goʊ tə wərk/ (by bus, train, car, etc.)

have a coffee /hæv ə 'kɑfi/

IN THE AFTERNOON

have lunch /hæv lʌntʃ/

finish work /'fɪnɪʃ wərk/

go home /goʊ hoʊm/

go shopping /goʊ 'ʃɑpɪŋ/

go to the gym /goʊ tə ðə dʒɪm/

IN THE EVENING

make dinner /meɪk 'dɪnər/

have dinner /hæv 'dɪnər/

do housework /du 'haʊswərk/

watch TV /wɑtʃ ti 'vi/

take a bath /teɪk ə bæθ/

go to bed /goʊ tə bɛd/

> 🔍 **make** and **do**
> **make** dinner / coffee **BUT** **do** housework, **do** homework
>
> **go** with **to** and **the**
> go **to the** gym, go **to the** movies
> go **to** work, go **to** school, go **to** bed
> go home **NOT** go to home

b 🔊 6.15 Listen and point to the picture.

🔈) *Lisa has lunch at one o'clock.* (*Picture six.*

ACTIVATION In pairs, describe Lisa's day. Say the times where there are clocks.

She gets up at a quarter to seven.   *She has breakfast.*

🔄 p.38

🔁 **Go online** to review the vocabulary for each lesson

Words and phrases to learn

1A 🔊 1.15

Hello.
Hi.
What's your name?
Nice to meet you.

A cappuccino, please.
A tea.
Yes.
No.
OK.
Thanks.
Sorry.
Just a minute.

Goodbye. / Bye.
See you on Friday.
See you tomorrow.

1B 🔊 1.31

Where are you from?
I'm from Spain.
Where's Izmir?
I think it's in Turkey.
It's a nice city.

I don't know.
Very good.
Wow!

2A 🔊 2.12

Excuse me.
Are these seats free?
Are you on vacation?
We're here on business.
What's that?
Have a nice day!
It's a beautiful city.
tourists
dogs
over there

2B 🔊 2.27

Who's he?
How old is he?
He's very good-looking.

How are you?
I'm fine.
This is Alex.
That's my bus.
This is my bus stop.

What class are you in?
What's your cell phone
    number?
See you later.

a bedroom
a kitchen
a yard

big
small

3A 🔊 3.9

Oh no!
Where's my cell phone?
Where are my glasses?

What is it?
What are they?

I think it's an ID card.
I think they're keys.

What's in your bag?
I have two credit cards.

3B 🔊 3.17

How much is this mug?
How much are these key
    chains?
They're twenty dollars.
A T-shirt, please.

Is this your cell phone?
Thank you very much.
You're welcome.

souvenirs
here
there

4A 🔊 4.12

Come in.
Be good.
Let's order pizza.

on the table
in my phone

Mom
Dad
a babysitter

What a nice card!
Can I see?
I remember.
maybe

4B 🔊 4.24

ma'am

an electric car
a sports car

easy to park
perfect

in her (my, your,…) opinion
Is the car for you?
I prefer this red car.
I love it!
Come with me.

a museum
a village
a motorcycle
famous

5A 🔊 5.10

a scientist
a doctor

sometimes
usually

I'm not hungry.
early
healthy
traditional
important
different
favorite

in a café
at home
at work

soup
green tea
toast
a lot of (fruit)

5B 🔊 5.20

a writer
a taxi driver
a British (American)
    company
a flight
traffic
a gate
in college
in high school

Do you want fish or pasta?
How's your pasta?
I need to go to the
    restroom.
What time do we arrive?
Keep the change.
Can I see your passport and
    boarding pass, please?
What a nice surprise!

6A 🔊 6.11

What does she do?
Where does he teach?
She's a journalist.
She doesn't wear glasses.
Her hair's blonde.
He's married to Lisa.

Great to see you.
intelligent
I know, right?
I love your shoes.

a banker
customers
dishes
a multinational company
meetings
Why? Because…

6B 🔊 6.19

Are you a morning person?
What time do you get up?
At eight o'clock.
He gets up at about 9:30.
feel tired

on the way to work
after work
every morning
then

a tour guide
an apartment
the subway
an omelet
It's delicious.

Regular and irregular verbs

COMMON REGULAR VERBS

answer /'ænsər/	answered /'ænsərd/
arrive /ə'raɪv/	arrived /ə'raɪvd/
ask /æsk/	asked /æskt/
book /bʊk/	booked /bʊkt/
call /kɔl/	called /kɔld/
carry /'kæri/	carried /'kærid/
change /tʃeɪndʒ/	changed /tʃeɪndʒd/
check in /tʃɛk 'ɪn/	checked in /tʃɛk 'ɪn/
clean /klin/	cleaned /klind/
close /kloʊz/	closed /kloʊzd/
cook /kʊk/	cooked /kʊkt/
cry /kraɪ/	cried /kraɪd/
decide /dɪ'saɪd/	decided /dɪ'saɪdəd/
finish /'fɪnɪʃ/	finished /'fɪnɪʃt/
hate /heɪt/	hated /'heɪtəd/
help /hɛlp/	helped /hɛlpt/
invite /ɪn'vaɪt/	invited /ɪn'vaɪtəd/
learn /lərn/	learned /lərnd/
like /laɪk/	liked /laɪkt/
listen /'lɪsn/	listened /'lɪsnd/
live /lɪv/	lived /lɪvd/
look /lʊk/	looked /lʊkt/
love /lʌv/	loved /lʌvd/
miss /mɪs/	missed /mɪst/
move /muv/	moved /muvd/
need /nid/	needed /'nidəd/
offer /'ɔfər/	offered /'ɔfərd/
open /'oʊpən/	opened /'oʊpənd/
pack /pæk/	packed /pækt/
paint /peɪnt/	painted /'peɪntəd/
park /pɑrk/	parked /pɑrkt/
pass /pæs/	passed /pæst/
play /pleɪ/	played /pleɪd/
rain /reɪn/	rained /reɪnd/
relax /rɪ'læks/	relaxed /rɪ'lækst/
rent /rɛnt/	rented /'rɛntəd/
snow /snoʊ/	snowed /snoʊd/
start /stɑrt/	started /'stɑrtəd/
stay /steɪ/	stayed /steɪd/
stop /stɑp/	stopped /stɑpt/
study /'stʌdi/	studied /'stʌdid/
talk /tɔk/	talked /tɔkt/
travel /'trævl/	traveled /'trævld/
turn /tərn/	turned /tərnd/
use /yuz/	used /yuzd/
wait /weɪt/	waited /'weɪtəd/
walk /wɔk/	walked /wɔkt/
want /wɑnt/	wanted /'wɑntəd/
wash /wɑʃ/	washed /wɑʃd/
watch /wɑtʃ/	watched /wɑtʃt/
work /wərk/	worked /wərkt/

COMMON IRREGULAR VERBS

be /bi/	
am /æm/ / is /ɪz/	was /wʌz/
are /ɑr/	were /wər/
buy /baɪ/	bought /bɔt/
do /du/	did /dɪd/
get /gɛt/	got /gɑt/
go /goʊ/	went /wɛnt/
have /hæv/	had /hæd/
leave /liv/	left /lɛft/
say /seɪ/	said /sɛd/
see /si/	saw /sɔ/
send /sɛnd/	sent /sɛnt/
sit /sɪt/	sat /sæt/
tell /tɛl/	told /toʊld/
write /raɪt/	wrote /roʊt/

Vowel sounds

		usual spelling	! but also
tree	ee	three meet	people key
	ea	please read	piece
	e	she we	
fish	i	his six is it	English
		big window	women gym
ear	eer	cheer	cereal
	ere	here we're	
	ear	near year	
cat	a	bag thanks man	
		black bad that	
egg	e	spell ten seven	bread friend
		twenty Mexico	breakfast
chair	air	airport repair	their careful
	ere	where there	
clock	o	not hot stop	what watch
		hospital	want
saw	al	talk walk	daughter
	aw	saw draw awful	water bought
horse	or	short important	four board
		door	
boot	oo	too food	juice two
	u*	excuse blue	you
	ew	new	

		usual spelling	! but also
bull	u	full sugar	woman could
	oo	good book	
		look cook	
tourist		A very unusual sound. euro Europe sure plural	
up	u	umbrella	son brother
		number brush	young
		husband but	
computer		Many different spellings. /ə/ is always unstressed. umbrella America famous about children	
bird	er	person verb	work word
	ir	thirsty girl	world
	ur	nurse Turkey	
owl	ou	out house	
		pound sound	
	ow	town down	
phone	o*	open close	window
		no hello	
	oa	coat	
car	ar	are park	heart
		start far	
train	a*	name late	eight they
	ai	email Spain	great
	ay	day say	
boy	oi	toilet noise	
	oy	boyfriend	
		enjoy	
bike	i*	I hi nice	buy
	y	bye my	
	igh	night right	

* especially before consonant + e

□ vowels □ vowels followed by /r/ □ diphthongs

Consonant sounds

		usual spelling	! but also
parrot	p	paper Peru sleep top	
	pp	stopped happy	
bag	b	board British remember job	
	bb	hobby	
key	c	color credit card	school
	k	look take	
	ck	back clock	
girl	g	go green big blog	
	gg	eggs	
flower	f	fifteen Friday wife	
	ph	photo phone	
	ff	office different	
vase	v	TV very have live seven five	of
tie	t	time tell start late	liked finished
	tt	letter butter	
dog	d	did drink study good	played cried
	dd	address middle	
snake	s	sit stand	science
	ss	glass actress	
	ce/ci	nice city	
zebra	z	zero Brazil	
	s	bags cars husband easy	
shower	sh	shop she Spanish finish	sugar sure
	ti	information reservation (ti + on)	
television	**An unusual sound.** usually usual		garage

		usual spelling	! but also
thumb	th	thing think tenth birthday month Thursday	
mother	th	the father this their that with	
chess	ch	children lunch	
	tch	watch kitchen	
	t (+ure)	picture	
jazz	j	Japan juice job	gym page
	dge	bridge	
leg	l	lamp listen plan table	
	ll	small umbrella	
right	r	red rice problem street	write wrong
	rr	terrible married	
witch	w	watch twenty word we	one
	wh	what white where	
yacht	y	yellow your yes you	
	before u	music university	
monkey	m	museum Monday September come	
	mm	summer swimming	
nose	n	nine never men fine	know
	nn	beginner dinner	
singer	ng	thing single doing going playing wrong	think thank
house	h	hello hi how he have hotel	who

☐ unvoiced   ☐ voiced

Go online to watch the Sound Bank videos

American English File

Third Edition

Starter

MULTI-PACK **A**
Student Book | Workbook

Christina Latham-Koenig
Clive Oxenden
Jerry Lambert

Paul Seligson and Clive Oxenden
are the original co-authors of
English File 1 and *English File 2*

OXFORD
UNIVERSITY PRESS

Contents

How to use your Workbook and Online Practice

IN CLASS

Student Book

Use your Student Book in class with your teacher.

American **English File**
Third Edition

AT HOME

ACTIVITIES   AUDIO   VIDEO   RESOURCES

ONLINE

Go to
americanenglishfileonline.com
and use the code on
your Access Card to
log into the Online
Practice.

Workbook

Practice **Grammar**, **Vocabulary**, and **Pronunciation** for every lesson.

Practice the **Practical English** for every episode.

Do the **Can you remember...?** exercises to check that you remember the Grammar, Vocabulary, and Pronunciation every two Files.

Online Practice

← Look again at the Grammar, Vocabulary, and Pronunciation from the Student Book before you do the Workbook exercises.

→ Listen to the audio for the Pronunciation exercises.

→ Use the Sound Bank video to practice English sounds.

← Watch the Practical English video before you do the exercises.

→ Use the interactive video for more Practical English practice.

→ Look again at the Grammar, Vocabulary, and Pronunciation if you have any problems.

Practice Reading, Listening, Speaking, and Writing.

A cappuccino, please

You say goodbye, and I say hello.
From the song Hello, Goodbye
by the Beatles

G verb *be* (singular): *I* and *you*   **V** numbers 0–10, days of the week   **P** /h/, /aɪ/, and /i/

1 GRAMMAR verb *be* (singular): *I* and *you*

a Write the sentences with contractions.

1 I am Tom.
   I'm Tom.

2 You are not in room 3.
   You aren't in room 3.

3 I am not Helen.
   _____

4 You are not a teacher.
   _____

5 I am Carlos.
   _____

6 You are in my class.
   _____

7 I am in room 4.
   _____

8 You are not Maria.
   _____

b Write negative ⊟ sentences or questions ?.

1 You're in my class. ⊟
   You aren't in my class.

2 You're a teacher. ?
   Are you a teacher?

3 I'm Jenny. ⊟
   _____

4 I'm in room 2. ⊟
   _____

5 I'm in room 4. ?
   _____

6 You're Dom. ?
   _____

7 I'm a student. ⊟
   _____

8 You're in room 7. ?
   _____ .

c Complete the conversations. Use contractions where possible.

1 A *Are you* _____ Andy?
   B No, *I'm* _____ Tony.

2 A Excuse me. _____
      in number 8?
   B Yes, _____ . I'm
      Anna Jones.

3 A Hello, _____ Amy.
   B Hi, _____ Steve.
      Nice to meet you.

4 A Hi, _____ Sofia.
      Are you Tomas?
   B No, _____ . I'm
      Max.

5 A Hello. _____
      Lisa Gomez?
   B Yes, _____ . Nice
      to meet you.

6 A Hi. _____ Ben.
   B Hi. _____ Rob.

7 A Excuse me. _____ in room 7?
  B No, _____. You're in room 8.

8 A Excuse me. _____ my teacher?
  B Yes, _____. I'm Peter Wilson.

2 VOCABULARY numbers 0–10, days of the week

a Write the numbers.

R U F O   f o u r
N E T   t e n
I N N E   n __ __ e
E O N   o __ __
T E R E H   t __ __ __ e
O W T   t __ __
G I T H E   e __ __ __ t
X I S   s __ __
E N V S E   s __ __ __ n
O Z R E   z __ __ o
V I E F   f __ __ e

b Write the numbers from **a** in the correct order.

0 _zero_
1 _____
2 _____
3 _____
4 _____
5 _____
6 _____
7 _____
8 _____
9 _____
10 _____

c Write the next day of the week.

1 Saturday Sunday _Monday_
2 Monday Tuesday _____
3 Thursday Friday _____
4 Sunday Monday _____
5 Friday Saturday _____
6 Tuesday Wednesday _____
7 Wednesday Thursday _____

d Answer the questions about you.

1 What's your name?
  _____

2 What class are you in?
  _____

3 What day is it today?
  _____

4 What days are your English classes?
  _____

3 PRONUNCIATION /h/, /aɪ/, and /i/

a 🔊 1.1 Listen and write the words in the chart.

~~five~~ Helen hello m**ee**t nice tea

1	2	3
house	b**i**ke	tr**ee**
	five	

b 🔊 1.2 Listen and check. Then listen again and repeat the words.

4 WORDS AND PHRASES TO LEARN

Complete the conversations with a word or phrase from the list.

Nice to meet you ~~Two cappuccinos, please~~
Sorry See you tomorrow Thanks What's your name

1 A _Two cappuccinos, please_ .
  B OK. Just a minute.

2 A Hi, I'm Helen.
  B Hi, I'm Rob. _____.

3 A Hello, I'm Sarah. _____?
  B Kento.

4 A Goodbye. _____.
  B No, Friday.
  A Oh yes, sorry. See you on Friday.

5 A I'm not John. I'm James.
  B _____.

6 A Bruno? Your tea.
  B _____.

Go online for more practice

1B World music

I am a citizen of the world.
Diogenes, Greek philosopher

G verb *be* (singular): *he, she, it*   **V** countries   **P** /ɪ/, /oʊ/, /s/, and /ʃ/

1 VOCABULARY countries

a Complete the crossword.

ACROSS →

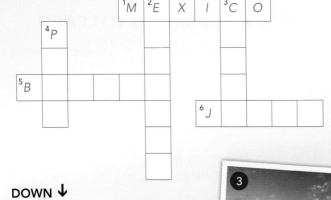

¹M	²E	X	I	³C	O

⁴P

⁵B

⁶J

DOWN ↓

b Complete the sentences with a country.

1 She's from Buenos Aires. She's from Ar*gentina*____.
2 He's from Seoul. He's from K_____.
3 I'm from Hanoi. I'm from V_____.
4 You're from Miami. You're from t____
   U_____ St_____.
5 She's from Toronto. She's from C_____.
6 He's from Istanbul. He's from T_____.
7 I'm from Santiago. I'm from C_____.
8 You're from Madrid. You're from S_____.
9 She's from Riyadh She's from S_____
   A_____.

2 GRAMMAR verb *be* (singular): *he, she, it*

a Complete the sentences with *He's, She's,* or *It's.*

1 *She's*____ from the
   United States.

2 *It's*____ from
   China.

3 _____ from
   Canada.

4 _____ from
   Saudi Arabia.

5 _____ from
   Mexico.

6 _____ from
   Japan.

7 _____ from
   Spain.

8 _____ from
   Korea.

b Complete the conversations with *'s*, *is*, or *isn't*.

1 A *Is*_____ Paulo from Argentina?
   B No, he *isn't*____. He _____ from Brazil.

2 A Where _____ Oaxaca? _____ it in Mexico?
   B Yes, it _____.

3 A _____ Yasmin in the Monday class?
   B No, she _____. She _____ in the Tuesday class.

4 A _____ your name Annie?
   B No, it _____. It _____ Anna.

c Write the questions. Then answer with the information in parentheses.

1 Robert Downey Jr. / from the US? (✔ New York)
   Is Robert Downey Jr. from the US _____?
   Yes, he is. He's from New York _____.

2 Kobe / in China? (✘ Japan)
   Is Kobe in China _____?
   No, it isn't. It's in Japan _____.

3 Salma Hayek / from Mexico? (✔ Veracruz)
   _____?
   _____.

4 Madrid / in Turkey? (✘ Spain)
   _____?
   _____.

5 Copacabana / in Brazil? (✔ Rio)
   _____?
   _____.

6 Busan / in Vietnam? (✘ Korea)
   _____?
   _____.

7 Gary Oldman / from England? (✔ London)
   _____?
   _____.

8 Toronto / in Saudi Arabia? (✘ Canada)
   _____?
   _____.

9 Javier Bardem / from Spain? (✔ Las Palmas)
   _____?
   _____.

10 Machu Picchu / in Chile? (✘ Peru)
   _____?
   _____.

d Answer the questions about you.

1 Are you from the United States?
   _____

2 Where are you from (city)?
   _____

3 Where is it?
   _____

3 PRONUNCIATION /ɪ/, /oʊ/, /s/, and /ʃ/

a ◉ 1.3 Listen and (circle) the word with a different sound.

🐟	fish	1 Brazil	(China)	**E**ngland
☎	ph**o**ne	2 hell**o**	Mexic**o**	tw**o**
🐍	**s**nake	3 **s**ix	**S**audi Arabia	**c**lassroom
ʃ	**sh**ower	4 Turki**sh**	**S**pain	**sh**e

b ◉ 1.3 Listen again and repeat the words.

4 WORDS AND PHRASES TO LEARN

Complete the conversations with a phrase from the list.

I don't know	I think she's from Spain	It's a nice city
~~Where are you from~~	Where's Lima	

1 A *Where are you from*?
   B I'm from the United States.
   A Where in the United States?
   B New York.
   A Wow! _____.

2 A Is Mercedes Peón from Mexico?
   B No, _____.

3 A Is Sapporo in China?
   B Sapporo? Sorry, _____.

4 A _____?
   B It's in Peru.

🕐 **Go online** for more practice

Practical English How do you spell it?

1 THE ALPHABET

a 🔊1.4 Listen and (circle) the letter with a different vowel sound.

i	1 D E (I) V
ɛ	2 E L N X
eɪ	3 A G J K
i	4 B H P D
ɛ	5 C F L S
eɪ	6 A H J Y
ʊ	7 O Q U W
ɛ	8 F T M S

b 🔊1.4 Listen again and repeat the letters.

c Say the letters in 1–5.

d 🔊1.5 Listen and check.

e 🔊1.6 Listen and write the words in the chart.

~~hello~~ help name please she spell Spain table teacher

i	ɛ	eɪ
1	2	3
tr**ee**	**e**gg	tr**ai**n
hello		

f 🔊1.7 Listen and check. Then listen again and repeat the words.

2 VOCABULARY the classroom

a Write the words.

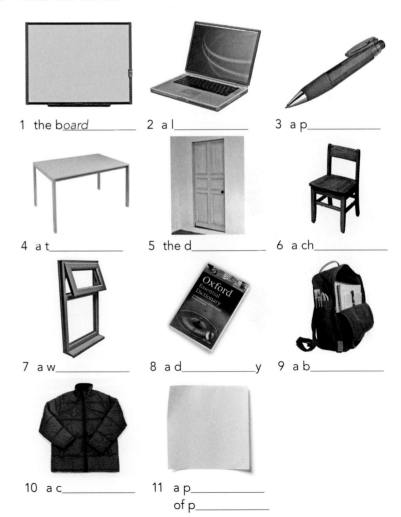

1 the b*oard*   2 a l_____   3 a p_____

4 a t_____   5 the d_____   6 a ch_____

7 a w_____   8 a d_____y   9 a b_____

10 a c_____   11 a p_____
                       of p_____

b Complete the classroom expressions with the words from the list.

books   Excuse   Go   ~~know~~   late   Look   Open
repeat   Sit   Stand   spell   understand

1 I don't *know*_____.
2 Sorry? Can you _____ that, please?
3 _____ at the board, please.
4 _____ your books.
5 I don't _____.
6 How do you _____ it?
7 _____ to page 9.
8 Close your _____.
9 _____ up, please.
10 _____ down.
11 _____ me. What's *obrigado* in English?
12 Sorry, I'm _____.

3   CHECKING INTO A HOTEL

Complete the conversation with the words from the list.

~~evening~~   last   name   reservation   spell   room

A Good ¹*evening*_____.
B Hello. I have a ²_____.
A What's your ³_____, please?
B Wendy Mahoney.
A How do you ⁴_____ your ⁵_____ name?
B M-A-H-O-N-E-Y.
A Thank you, Ms. Mahoney. You're in ⁶_____ 261.
B Thanks.

4   BOOKING A TABLE

Match the questions in the conversation to answers a–e below.

A Good morning. How can I help you?
B ¹ *b*
A What time?
B ² ____
A OK, that's fine. What's your name, please?
B ³ ____
A OK. How many people?
B ⁴ ____
A Thank you, Mr. Anderson. So, a table for three on Tuesday at seven?
B ⁵ ____

a Three.
b ~~A table for Tuesday evening, please.~~
c Yes, that's great. Thanks.
d Steve Anderson.
e Seven o'clock.

5   USEFUL PHRASES

Complete the conversations with a phrase from the list.

A table for tomorrow, please   Good morning
~~How can I help you~~   How do you spell it
I have a reservation   Sorry   Thank you   That's right

1 **A** Good morning. ¹*How can I help you*?
  B My name's Kim Chopra. ²_____ for a room for tonight.
  A OK – Chopra. ³_____?
  B C-H-O-P-R-A.
  A That's C-H-O-P-R-A?
  B ⁴_____.
  A OK, you're in room 49.

2 **A** ⁵_____, The Green Tree restaurant. How can I help you?
  B ⁶_____ – for four people.
  A OK. What time?
  B 7:30.
  A ⁷_____?
  B 7:30.
  A ⁸_____.

Go online to practice the Practical English phrases   Go online to check your progress

Our true nationality is mankind.
H.G. Wells, British writer

G verb *be* (plural): *we, you, they* **V** nationalities **P** /dʒ/, /tʃ/, and /ʃ/

1 VOCABULARY nationalities

Complete the puzzle. What's the mystery word?

¹S	P	A	N	I	S	H

1 Maria's from Spain.
She's **S** panis **h**.

2 Kentaro's from Japan.
He's **J** ____ **e**.

3 Emma's from the UK.
She's **B** ____ **h**.

4 Bianca's from Brazil.
She's **Br** ____ **n**.

5 Jae-won's from Korea.
He's **South K** ____ **n**.

6 Meiling's from China.
She's **Ch** ____ **e**.

7 Jorge's from Peru.
He's **P** ____ **n**.

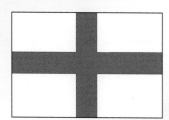

8 William's from England.
He's **E** ____ **h**.

9 Daniela's from Mexico.
She's **M** ____ **n**.

10 Bao's from Vietnam.
He's **V** ____ **e**.

11 Sarah's from Canada.
She's **C** ____ **n**.

12 Mike's from the United States.
He's **Am** ____ **n**.

13 Faisal's from Saudi Arabia.
He's **S** ____ **i**.

2 PRONUNCIATION /dʒ/, /tʃ/, and /ʃ/

a 🔊 2.1 Listen and write the words in the chart.

~~Argentina~~   Chilean   Chinese   dictionary
Japanese   just   teacher   Turkish

1 jazz	2 chess	3 shower
Argentina		

b 🔊 2.2 Listen and check. Then listen again and repeat the words.

3 GRAMMAR verb be (plural): we, you, they

a Write affirmative ➕ and negative ➖ sentences with *be*. Use contractions.

1 we / from Korea ✓ Vietnam ✗
   We're from Korea. We aren't from Vietnam.

2 you / teachers ✓ students ✗
   _____

3 they / Chinese ✓ Japanese ✗
   _____

4 we / from Mexico ✓ Brazil ✗
   _____

5 you / in class 3 ✓ class 2 ✗
   _____

6 they / from Saudi Arabia ✓ Turkey ✗
   _____

7 she / room 4 ✓ room 5 ✗
   _____

8 I / Peruvian ✓ Chilean ✗
   _____

b Write the sentences with pronouns. Use contractions.

1 Juan and I are from Spain.
   We're from Spain.

2 Sara and Mikel are in class 6.
   _____

3 Marina's on vacation.
   _____

4 Rodrigo's from Brazil.
   _____

5 Yasuo and I are here on business.
   _____

6 Toronto is in Canada.
   _____

c Re-order the words to make questions.

1 dogs   they   are   your
   Are they your dogs _____?

2 class   in   1   are   they
   _____?

3 they   England   from   are
   _____?

4 Brazilian   Fernanda   is
   _____?

5 in   Ankara   is   Turkey
   _____?

d Match the answers to the questions in **c**.

a _4_   Yes, she is.
b ____   No, they're in class 2.
c ____   No, they aren't.
d ____   Yes, it is.
e ____   Yes, they're from London.

e Answer the questions about your class.

1 Are you American?
   No, we aren't. We're _____.
2 Where are you from?
   _____.
3 What room are you in?
   _____.

4 WORDS AND PHRASES TO LEARN

Complete the missing words in the conversations.

1 A Excuse me. A_re_____ these seats
      fr_ee_____?
   B Yes, they are. Please sit down.
   A Thanks.

2 A A_____ y_____ o_____
      v_____?
   B Yes, we are. We're from Canada.

3 A Your cappuccino.
   B Thanks.
   A H_____ a n_____ d_____!

4 A Are you on business?
   B No, we aren't. We're t_____. We're
      on vacation.

🔵 **Go online** for more practice

G *Wh-* and *How* questions with *be* | **V** numbers 11–100, phone numbers | **P** understanding numbers

1 GRAMMAR *Wh-* and *How* questions with *be*

a Complete the questions with a question word and *are* or *'s*.

1 A <u>Who's</u> Sarah Lawson?
  B She's my English teacher.

2 A _____ the concert?
  B It's on Monday.

3 A _____ she from?
  B She's from Spain.

4 A _____ your phone number?
  B It's 818-555-9284.

5 A _____ you from?
  B I'm from Brazil.

6 A _____ Mari and Laura?
  B They're on vacation in Boston.

7 A _____ old _____ Pedro?
  B He's 27.

8 A _____ your address?
  B It's 47 Bank Street.

9 A _____ you?
  B I'm fine, thanks. And you?

b Complete the conversation. Write the questions.

A [1] <u>What's your name</u> ?
B My name's Brian Halley.
A [2] _____ ?
B H-A-L-L-E-Y.
A Thank you. [3] _____ ?
B I'm from the United States.
A [4] _____ ?
B It's 64 Bond Street, New York City.
A Thank you. [5] _____ ?
B My phone number is 784-2913.
A [6] _____ ?
B It's b.halley@gomail.com.
A Thank you. [7] _____ ?
B I'm 23.
A [8] _____ ?
B No, I'm not. I'm single.

c Answer the questions about you.

1 What's your phone number?
  _____

2 What's your zip code?
  _____

3 Are you single?
  _____

4 What's your last name?
  _____

5 What's your address?
  _____

6 How old are you?
  _____

7 What's your email?
  _____

8 How do you spell your last name?
  _____

2 VOCABULARY numbers 11–100, phone numbers

a Complete the numbers.

1 **20** t _w_ _e_ nt _y_

2 **15** f _ _ t _ _ n

3 **90** ni _ _ t _

4 **70** s _ v _ nt _

5 **12** t _ _ lv _

6 **100** a hu _ _ r _ _

7 **80** ei _ _ t _

8 **11** e _ _ v _ _

9 **40** fo _ t _

10 **13** th _ r _ _ _ n

11 **60** si _ t _

b Write the numbers.

1 forty-seven   _47_
2 nineteen   ____
3 thirty-eight   ____
4 fifty-nine   ____
5 seventy-two   ____
6 fourteen   ____
7 ninety-one   ____
8 sixteen   ____
9 twenty-three   ____
10 eighteen   ____

3 PRONUNCIATION understanding numbers

a 2.3 Listen and complete the phone numbers.

1 9 ▢ ▢ - ▢ 2 ▢ - 7 ▢ 1
2 ▢ ▢ 4 - 5 ▢ ▢ - ▢ ▢ ▢ 1
3 ▢ 5 ▢ - ▢ ▢ 2 - ▢ 4 ▢ ▢

b 2.3 Listen again and repeat the phone numbers.

c 2.4 Listen and write the numbers.

1 _17_ Lake Road
2 I'm ____.
3 anne.davis____@gmail.com
4 You're in room ____.
5 90____ 1

d 2.4 Listen again and repeat the numbers.

4 WORDS AND PHRASES TO LEARN

Complete the missing words in the conversations.

1 A Wh_o's_____ she_____?
   B Jenny.
   A H_____ o_____ is she?
   B She's 21.
   A W_____ c_____ is she in?
   B She's in my class.
   A She's very g_____-l_____.

2 A Hi, Tom. H_____ a_____
      y_____?
   B I'm f_____, thanks.
   A Th_____ is Jenny.
   B Nice to meet you.
   C Nice to meet you, too. That's my bus.
      S_____ y_____ l_____.

3 A W_____ are you f_____?
   B Miami.
   A Where's Miami?
   B It's in the southern part of Florida.

Go online for more practice   Go online to check your progress

Where are my keys?

Own only what you can carry with you.
Aleksandr Solzhenitsyn, Russian writer

G singular and plural nouns, *a / an*   **V** small things   **P** /z/ and /s/, plural endings

1 VOCABULARY small things

Complete the crossword.

DOWN ↓

ACROSS →

2 GRAMMAR singular and plural nouns, *a / an*

a Write *a* or *an*.

1 *a* camera
2 *an* umbrella
3 ____ book
4 ____ watch
5 ____ email
6 ____ country
7 ____ city
8 ____ key
9 ____ address
10 ____ laptop
11 ____ debit card

b Write the plurals of the words in **a**.

1 *cameras*
2 _____
3 _____
4 _____
5 _____
6 _____
7 _____
8 _____
9 _____
10 _____
11 _____

c Write questions and answers.

1 _What is it_____?
  _It's a dictionary_____.

2 _____?
  _____.

 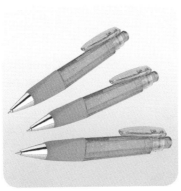

3 _____?
  _____.

4 _____?
  _____.

5 _____?
  _____.

6 _____?
  _____.

7 _____?
  _____.

8 _____?
  _____.

d What's in your bag? Write five things.

_a wallet_____
_____
_____
_____
_____

3 PRONUNCIATION /z/ and /s/, plural endings

a 🔊 3.1 Listen and repeat the words and sounds.

🦓 **z**ebra	1 name**s**	bag**s**
🐍 **s**nake	2 book**s**	student**s**
/ɪz/	3 address**es**	purs**es**

b 🔊 3.2 Listen and (circle) three words with /ɪz/.

pieces classes coats glasses
laptops pencils phones wallets

c 🔊 3.2 Listen again and repeat the words.

4 WORDS AND PHRASES TO LEARN

Complete the conversations with a phrase from the list.

~~Oh no~~ What are they What's in your bag
Where are my glasses

1 A Where's your bag?
  B _Oh no_____! It's in the car!

2 A _____?
  B They're in your bag.

3 A Excuse me, sir. _____?
  B I have a wallet, a book, and an umbrella.

4 A _____?
  B I think they're credit cards.

🔵 **Go online** for more practice

3B Souvenirs

G this / that / these / those **V** souvenirs **P** /ð/, sentence rhythm

A photograph is a souvenir of life.
Deborah Smith, British translator

1 VOCABULARY souvenirs

Match the words in the list to the pictures.

cap key chain map mug
postcard toy T-shirt sunglasses

1 *cap*

2 _____

3 _____

4 _____

5 _____

6 _____

7 _____

8 _____

2 GRAMMAR this / that / these / those

a Re-order the words to make sentences or questions.

1 these bags are
   *These are bags*_____.

2 is what that
   _____?

3 book isn't this your
   _____.

4 postcards my those are
   _____.

5 your are keys those
   _____?

6 my aren't photos these
   _____.

7 that friend is your
   _____?

8 from where this is
   _____?

b Complete the sentences with *this*, *that*, *these*, or *those*.

1 *That*_____'s a beautiful picture!

2 **A** Is _____ a Manchester
     United shirt?
   B No, it's Manchester City.

3 _____ are $10.

16

4 **A** Are _____ your keys?
   B Yes, they are. Thank you!

5 Look! _____'s Martin from our English class.

6 Wow. _____ are good glasses!

7 **A** I like _____ cap.
   B Yes, it's great.

8 **A** Are _____ toys $5?
   B No, they're $10.

c Complete the conversations with typical souvenirs from your country and the price.

1 **A** Excuse me. What are those?
   B They're *key chains*_____.
   A How much are they?
   B They're *$3.50*_____.

2 **A** Excuse me. What's that?
   B It's a(n) _____.
   A How much is it?
   B It's _____.

3 **A** Excuse me. What are these?
   B They're _____.
   A How much are they?
   B They're _____.

4 **A** Excuse me. What's this?
   B It's a(n) _____.
   A How much is it?
   B It's _____.

3 PRONUNCIATION /ð/, sentence rhythm

a 🔊 3.3 Listen and complete the sentences.

1 *This*_____ is *my*_____ *mother*_____.
2 _____ _____ over there?
3 _____ are my keys.
4 _____ are your _____.
5 Is _____ your _____?

b 🔊 3.3 Listen again and repeat the sentences. Copy the rhythm.

4 WORDS AND PHRASES TO LEARN

Complete the missing words in the conversations.

1 **A** H*ow*_____ m*uch*_____ a*re*_____ these key chains?
   B They're $2.50.

2 **A** I_____ this y_____ phone?
   B Oh yes, it is. Thank you very much.
   A Y_____ w_____.

3 **A** Is that your bag th_____?
   B No, my bag's h_____.

4 **A** H_____ m_____ i_____ th_____ mug?
   B It's $5.00.

🔴 **Go online** for more practice

Practical English   Can I have an orange juice, please?

understanding prices, buying lunch   **P** /ʊr/, /s/, and /k/

1 UNDERSTANDING PRICES

a Write the numbers.

1 *one* cent   2 _____ dollars

3 _____ cents   4 _____ euros

5 _____ pence (p)   6 _____ pounds

b Complete the prices.

1 €75   seventy-five *euros* _____

2 £21.99   twenty-one _____ ninety-nine

3 $38.50   thirty-eight _____ and fifty cents

4 40p   forty _____

5 €11.60   eleven _____ sixty

6 £2.50   two _____ fifty

c Write the prices.

1 *forty-five cents* _____   2 _____

3 _____   4 _____

5 _____   6 _____

7 _____   8 _____

2 PRONUNCIATION /ʊr/, /s/, and /k/

a 🔊 3.4 Listen and circle the word with a different sound.

ʊr	**tou**rist	1 (**jour**nalist)	**su**re	**Eur**opean	
s	**s**nake	2 pen**c**il	pri**c**e	**c**offee	
k	**k**ey	3 **c**ard	**c**ent	**c**amera	

b 🔊 3.4 Listen again and repeat the words.

c 🔊 3.5 Write the words in the chart. Listen and check. Then listen again and repeat the words.

~~c~~ity   ~~c~~lass   **c**lose   jui**c**e   ni**c**e   pi**c**ture

s	**s**nake	1 *city*
k	**k**ey	2 *class*

3 BUYING LUNCH

a Read the menu and write the prices.

MENU

FOOD

Steak or fish pie
$10.50

Cheese, tuna, or chicken sandwiches
$5.25

Burger
$8.00

Chicken salad
$8.50

DRINK

Mineral water
$1.25

Orange juice
$2.60

Soda
$2.80

Coffee / Tea
$1.70

1 **A** How much is a steak pie?
   B It's _$10.50_____ .

2 **A** How much is a burger?
   B It's _____ .

3 **A** How much is a chicken salad?
   B It's _____ .

4 **A** How much is an orange juice?
   B It's _____ .

5 **A** How much is a coffee?
   B It's _____ .

b Complete the conversations.

a Hi, yes. A chicken salad and a soda, please.
b Here you are.
c How much is it?
d Thanks.
e Can I have a burger and a mineral water, please?
f Here's your change.
g Yes, a mineral water.
h No, thanks.
i Anything else?

1

Server	Who's next?
Aya	[1]_Hi. A chicken salad and a soda, please._____
Server	Anything else?
Aya	[2]_____
Server	Ice and lemon with your drinks?
Aya	[3]_____
Server	There you go. That's $11.30.
Aya	[4]_____
Server	Thanks. Here's your change.
Aya	[5]_____

2

Assistant	Can I help you?
Dan	Yes. [6]_____
Assistant	Of course. [7]_____
Dan	No, thanks.
Assistant	There you go.
Dan	Thanks. [8]_____
Assistant	$9.25.
Dan	Here you are.
Assistant	Thanks. [9]_____
Dan	Thank you. Have a nice day.

4 USEFUL PHRASES

Complete the missing words and phrases in the conversations.

1 **A** Seb! Hi, how are you?
   B I'm f_ine_____ , th_anks_____ .

2 **A** That's $12.75, please.
   B Here you are.
   A Thanks. H_____ your ch_____ .

3 **A** C_____ I h_____ a cheese sandwich, please?
   B Yes, of course. Anything else?

4 **A** H_____ m_____ is it?
   B €8.70.

5 **A** We can have lunch together today.
   B Sure! Gr_____ i_____ .

6 **A** A_____ e_____ ?
   B And a tea, please.

4A Meet the family

> Happiness is having a large, loving family, ... in another city.
> *George Burns, American comedian*

G possessive adjectives, possessive 's   **V** people and family   **P** /ʌ/, /æ/, and /ɔ/

1 VOCABULARY people and family

a Complete the chart.

singular	plural
boy	¹ *boys*
²	girls
woman	³
man	⁴
⁵	friends
child	⁶
person	⁷

b Complete the sentences.

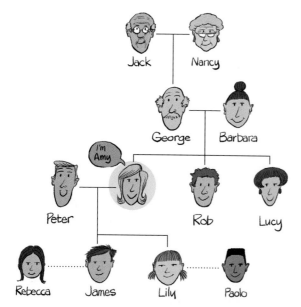

1 I'm Amy. I'm Peter's w*ife*_____.
2 George is my f_____ .
3 Peter's my h_____.
4 Barbara's my m_____.
5 George and Barbara are my p_____.
6 Lily's my d_____.
7 Rob's my br_____.
8 James is my s_____.
9 Rebecca is James's g_____.
10 Lucy's my s_____.
11 Paolo is Lily's b_____.
12 Jack is my gr_____.
13 Nancy is my gr_____.
14 Jack and Nancy are my gr_____.

2 GRAMMAR possessive adjectives, possessive 's

a Complete the chart.

subject pronoun	possessive adjective
I	¹ *my*
² *you*	your
he	³
⁴	her
it	⁵
⁶	our
you	⁷
⁸	their

b Complete the sentences with a possessive adjective.

1 That's *my*_____ laptop!

2 This is _____ daughter.

3 What's _____ name?

4 Look at _____ coat.

5 Here's _____ coffee, sir.

6 This is _____ new house.

7 It's a Mexican restaurant. _____ name is Diego's.

8 _____ names are Emily and Joel.

c Complete the sentences.

1 Carmen is Diego's sister.
Diego is _Carmen's brother_ .

2 Charlotte is Peter's wife.
Peter is _____.

3 Mark is Angelina's brother.
Angelina is _____.

4 Richard is Maria's father.
Maria is _____.

5 Ana is Paulo's mother.
Paulo is _____.

6 Omar is Laila's husband.
Laila is _____.

7 Sarah is Michael's daughter.
Michael is _____.

8 Roberto is Luisa's son.
Luisa is _____.

d Look at the 's in the sentences.
Check (✓) Possessive or *is*.

	Possessive	*is*
1 Mark's wife is Brazilian.	✓	
2 Angela's on vacation.		✓
3 Those are Amy's cats.		
4 It's a great phone.		
5 This is my brother's room.		
6 Jennifer's in Seoul.		
7 What's your name?		
8 Peter's son is twelve.		

e Think of five people. Who are they?
Write a sentence about them.

Anna's my sister.
Ali's my friend's brother.

1 _____
2 _____
3 _____
4 _____
5 _____

3 PRONUNCIATION /ʌ/, /æ/, and /ə/

a 🔊 4.1 Listen and (circle) the word with a different sound.

⬆ up	1 br**o**ther M**o**nday (ph**o**ne) S**u**nday
⬆ up	2 s**o**n Th**ur**sday h**u**sband m**o**ther
🐱 cat	3 f**a**mily n**a**me th**a**nks s**a**ndwich
💻 computer	4 m**e**n grandpar**e**nt childr**e**n wom**a**n

b 🔊 4.1 Listen again and repeat the words.

4 WORDS AND PHRASES TO LEARN

Complete the conversations with a phrase from the list.

Be good   ~~Come in~~   in my phone   Let's order pizza
on the table   What a nice card

1 A Hello, Tomo! _Come in_ .
B Thank you.

2 A Where's your phone?
B It's _____.

3 A What's Alice's number?
B Just a minute. It's _____.

4 A Gus, this is Ella. She's your babysitter
today. _____.
B OK, Mom.

5 A _____.
B Good idea. I love pizza.

6 A _____!
B It's from my sister.

I couldn't find the car of my dreams, so I built it myself.
Ferdinand Porsche, Austrian engineer

G adjectives **V** colors and common adjectives **P** /ɑr/ and /ɔr/, linking

1 VOCABULARY colors and common adjectives

a Complete the sentences with a color.

1 E L U B
My car is *blue*_____.

2 C A B L K
Her umbrella is _____.

3 N O W B R
His bag is _____.

4 D E R
Gabriel's T-shirt is _____.

5 H E T I W
The board is _____.

6 N E R G E
Their house is _____.

7 W E Y L O L
Amelia's coat is _____.

8 O G N R E A
His cap is _____.

b Complete the sentences with the opposite of the **bold** word.

1 Our house isn't **small**.
It's *big*_____.

2 My car isn't **fast**.
It's _____.

3 Yulia's phone isn't **cheap**.
It's _____.

4 His laptop isn't **new**.
It's _____.

5 Tim's name isn't **long**.
It's _____.

6 Their teacher isn't **bad**.
She's _____.

7 My car isn't **clean**.
It's _____.

8 My cat isn't **ugly**.
It's _____.

9 This exercise isn't **easy**.
It's _____.

c Complete the words.

1 That house is very o*ld*_____!

2 Is this bag e_____?

3 This book is very l_____.

4 The English test is d_____.

5 Tom's sister is b_____.

6 Those phones are ch_____.

2 GRAMMAR adjectives

a Re-order the words to make sentences.

1 I a car have blue
  I have a blue car .

2 a it's expensive camera very
  _____ .

3 good they're children very
  _____ .

4 a cheap that's phone
  _____ .

5 has a my house red door
  _____ .

6 a day it's beautiful
  _____ .

7 a new tablet I have
  _____ .

8 watch this nice is a
  _____ .

b Rewrite the sentences.

1 The car is very slow.
  It's a *very slow car* .

2 These exercises are very easy.
  They're _____ .

3 This movie is very long.
  It's a _____ .

4 The windows are green.
  They're _____ .

5 Those umbrellas are very big.
  They're _____ .

6 That phone is old.
  It's an _____ .

7 The people are nice.
  They're _____ .

8 The dictionary is Spanish.
  It's a _____ .

3 PRONUNCIATION /ɑr/ and /ɔr/, linking

a 4.2 Listen and circle the word with a different sound.

ɑr car	1 p**ar**k **are** color
ɔr horse	2 b**oar**d c**ar** d**oor**
ɑr car	3 M**ar**k f**our** l**ar**ge
ɔr horse	4 ID c**ar**d **or**ange sh**or**t

b 4.2 Listen again and repeat the words.

c 4.3 Listen and write the phrases.

1 _____
2 _____
3 _____
4 _____
5 _____

d 4.3 Listen again and repeat the phrases.

4 WORDS AND PHRASES TO LEARN

Complete the conversation with phrases from the list.

Come with me   easy to park   I love it
in my opinion   I prefer this red car   ~~Is the car for you~~

A ¹*Is the car for you* ?
B No, it's for my daughter.
C Yes, it's for me. It's my birthday.
A What about this green car here? It's small
  and it's ² _____ .
B Well, ³ _____ , it's perfect for you.
C But I don't like green. ⁴ _____ .
B The red one? That's a sports car!
C Yes, but it's my birthday and ⁵ _____ !
  It's a beautiful car. How much is it?
A ⁶ _____ , ma'am.

A big breakfast?

Eat breakfast like a king, lunch like a prince, and dinner like a poor man.
an old saying / Anonymous

G simple present ⊞ and ⊟: *I, you, we, they* **V** food and drink **P** word stress, /dʒ/ and /g/

1 VOCABULARY food and drink

a Complete the crossword.

DOWN ↓

ACROSS →

b What do they have for dinner? Complete the words.

1 f _i_ _s_ _h_
2 s _a_ _l_ _a_ _d_
3 t __ a

4 p _ _ _ _ a
5 v _ _ _ _ _ _ _ _ _ s
6 m _ _ _ k

7 m _ _ _ t
8 p _ _ _ _ _ _ _ s
9 w _ _ _ _ r

10 a s _ _ _ _ _ _ _ _ h
11 ch _ _ _ _ _ _ _ e
12 or _ _ _ _ e j _ _ _ e

2 PRONUNCIATION /dʒ/ and /g/

a 🔊5.1 Listen and <u>underline</u> the stressed syllable.

<u>cer</u>|e|al po|ta|toes vege|ta|bles cho|colate
break|fast sand|wich yo|gurt

b 🔊5.1 Listen again and repeat the words.

c 🔊5.2 Listen and (circle) the word with a different sound.

 jazz	1 (get) oran**g**e **j**uice
 **g**irl	2 e**gg**s **J**apan su**g**ar
 jazz	3 pa**g**e **g**reen ve**ge**tables
 **g**irl	4 **g**ood yo**g**urt Ar**g**entina

d 🔊5.2 Listen again and repeat the words.

3 GRAMMAR simple present ⊞ and ⊟: I, you, we, they

a Complete the sentences with the ⊞ or ⊟ of the verb in parentheses.

1 My friends _don't eat_ healthy food. (⊟ eat)
2 I _____ breakfast at home. (⊟ have)
3 You _____ a lot of water. (⊞ drink)
4 I _____ fish. (⊞ like)
5 I _____ coffee in the afternoon. (⊟ drink)
6 We _____ a salad for lunch. (⊞ have)
7 I don't drink tea because I _____ it. (⊟ like)
8 My children _____ a lot of fruit. (⊞ eat)

b Complete the texts with the correct form of the verbs from the list.

drink ~~have~~ not have not like

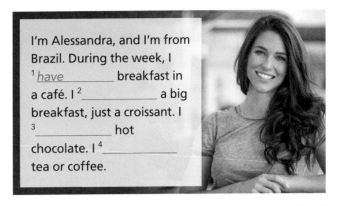

I'm Alessandra, and I'm from Brazil. During the week, I ¹ _have_ breakfast in a café. I ² _____ a big breakfast, just a croissant. I ³ _____ hot chocolate. I ⁴ _____ tea or coffee.

eat not drink not have

My name is Tim and I'm from Canada. I ⁵ _____ breakfast with my family during the week, but on weekends we sit down together. We ⁶ _____ a very big breakfast: eggs, cheese, cereal, and bread. I ⁷ _____ tea, so I have coffee.

c What's your favorite meal of the day? Where do you have it? What food and drink do you have?

My favorite meal of the day is _____
_____
_____
_____
_____

4 WORDS AND PHRASES TO LEARN

Complete the missing words in the sentences.

1 I don't eat breakfast because I'm not h_ungry_ in the morning.
2 Some doctors and scientists think breakfast is an i_____ meal.
3 Breakfast is my f_____ meal.
4 I have lunch e_____ – at 11:30.
5 I sometimes have breakfast i_____ a c_____.
6 Rice, fruit, and miso soup is a tr_____ breakfast in Japan.
7 I usually have breakfast a_____ h_____.

G simple present ?: *I, you, we, they*   **V** common verb phrases 1   **P** /w/ and /v/, sentence rhythm and linking

1 GRAMMAR simple present ?: *I, you, we, they*

a Complete the interview with the questions.

> Are you married?   What airline do you work for?
> Do you have children?   ~~What's your name?~~
> Do you like your job?   Where are you from?

Interview with **a flight attendant**

1 *What's your name?*

My name's Lucas.

2 _____

I'm from Rio de Janeiro. It's a big, beautiful city.

3 _____

Yes, I am. My wife's Canadian. Her name is Celia.

4 _____

Yes, we do. We have a little girl. Her name's Bianca. She's three.

5 _____

I work for Gol, the Brazilian airline.

6 _____

Yes, I do. I work with my friends, and I speak to a lot of new people every day. It's very interesting.

b Complete the questions.

1 A We don't live in an apartment.
  B *Do you live* _____ in a house?

2 A I don't want a newspaper.
  B _____ a magazine?

3 A They don't like dogs.
  B _____ cats?

4 A I don't have a camera.
  B _____ a phone?

5 A I don't drink tea.
  B _____ coffee?

6 A We don't have breakfast.
  B _____ lunch?

7 A I don't need a new phone.
  B _____ tablet?

c Complete the conversation with *do* or *don't*.

Jon	[1]*Do* _____ you have a car, Rachel?
Rachel	No, I [2]_____.
Jon	Oh. [3]_____ you work in Vancouver?
Rachel	Yes, I [4]_____. I work in a bank.
Waiter	Excuse me. [5]_____ you want a coffee, sir?
Jon	Yes, please.
Waiter	And you, ma'am?
Rachel	No, thanks. I [6]_____ like coffee.
Jon	They have tea. [7]_____ you like tea?
Rachel	Yes, I [8]_____.
Waiter	OK. One coffee and one tea.

d Answer the questions about you.

1 Do you work or study?

_____

2 Where do you work / study?

_____

3 Do you have a car?

_____

4 Do you like coffee?

_____

2 VOCABULARY common verb phrases 1

Write the verbs.

| drink | eat | go | ~~have~~ | have | listen | like | live |
| need | read | speak | study | want | watch | work |

1 _have_ lunch

2 _____ cats

3 _____ milk

4 _____
Chinese

5 _____
Mexican food

6 _____
magazines

7 _____ a
new car

8 _____ to
Brazilian music

9 _____ in
a bank

10 _____ in a
house

11 _____ TV in
the evening

12 _____ three
dogs

13 _____
Spanish

14 _____ to
English classes

15 _____
a coffee

3 PRONUNCIATION /w/ and /v/, sentence rhythm and linking

a 🔊 5.3 Listen and write the words in the correct column.

🪄	🌷
witch	**v**ase

b 🔊 5.3 Listen again and repeat the words.

c 🔊 5.4 Listen and complete the sentences.

1 Do you _want_ _____ _a_
sandwich?

2 I _____ _____ brother and
_____ _____teacher.

3 I _____ _____
_____ house _____
_____ small city.

4 I _____ _____
_____ TV.

d 🔊 5.4 Listen again and repeat the sentences. Copy the rhythm.

4 WORDS AND PHRASES TO LEARN

Complete the conversations with a phrase from the list.

~~Can I see your passport and boarding pass, please~~   Do you want fish or pasta
keep the change   What time do we arrive

1 A _Can I see your passport and boarding pass, please?_
B Yes, here you are.

2 A Excuse me, ma'am.
_____?
B Fish, please.

3 A _____?
B In 15 minutes, sir.

4 A That's $4.75, please.
B Here you are – _____.

🔵 Go online for more practice

Practical English What time is it?

telling the time **V** the time, saying how you feel **P** /ɑ/, silent consonants

1 TELLING THE TIME

Complete the conversations.

1 A What _time_ is it?
  B It's _quarter_ to eleven.

2 A It's ten to five. What _____ your train?
  B _____ five fifteen.

3 A What time is _____?
  B It's quarter _____ four.

4 A Hello. I'm _____ I'm late.
  B You're two hours late – _____ 11:30!

2 VOCABULARY the time

a Complete the times.

1 It's two _thirty_____.

2 It's eight _____.

3 It's _____ fifteen.

4 It's a _____ to six.

5 It's eleven _____.

6 It's twelve _____.

7 It's _____ after nine.

8 It's _____ to seven.

9 It's _____ after five.

10 It's _____ to twelve.

11 It's _____ after three.

12 It's _____ to four.

b ◆)5.5 Listen and draw the times on the clocks.

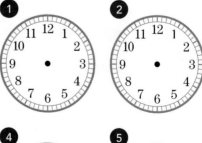
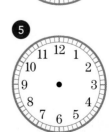
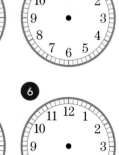

3 PRONUNCIATION /ɑ/, silent consonants

a 🔊 5.6 Listen and (circle) the word with a different sound.

1	what	(small)	hot
2	mother	sorry	not
3	Oxford	coffee	son
4	watch	old	chocolate
5	laptop	want	now

b 🔊 5.6 Listen again and repeat the words.

c 🔊 5.7 Listen and cross out the silent consonants in these words.

1 half   5 two
2 hour   6 Wednesday
3 know   7 what
4 listen   8 write

d 🔊 5.7 Listen again and repeat the words.

4 VOCABULARY saying how you feel

Complete the sentences.

1 He's *hot*_____.

2 He's _____.

3 She's _____.   4 She's _____.

5 He's _____.

5 USEFUL PHRASES

Complete the missing words and phrases in the conversation.

A Hi, Adam. I'm ¹*really*_____ *sorry*_____ I'm late. What time's the movie?

B ²D_____ w_____. It's OK – it's at seven thirty. It's only seven ten.

* * *

A ³W_____ a gr_____ movie!

B Yes – fantastic! Do you want to go to a coffee shop now?

A But it's ten thirty. It's ⁴I_____ and I'm ⁵t_____.

B ⁶C_____ o_____. I know a really good coffee shop near here.

A Oh, OK. ⁷L_____ g_____.

6A A school reunion

Find a job you like and you
add five days to every week.
H. Jackson Brown, Jr., American author

G simple present: *he, she, it*　**V** jobs and places of work　**P** third person *-es*, sentence rhythm

1 GRAMMAR simple present: *he, she, it*

a Look at the chart and complete the sentences.

	Amy	Luis
live in a big city	✗	✓
like cats	✓	✗
listen to pop music	✓	✗
speak Spanish	✗	✓
drink tea	✗	✓

1 Amy *doesn't live* in a big city.
2 She _____ cats.
3 She _____ to pop music.
4 She _____ Spanish.
5 She _____ tea.
6 Luis _____ in a big city.
7 He _____ cats.
8 He _____ to pop music.
9 He _____ Spanish.
10 He _____ tea.

b Complete the text with the correct form of the verbs in parentheses.

Ryan is an English teacher in Mexico. He
¹*lives* _____ (live) in Mexico City, and he
² _____ (work) in a language school
there. He ³ _____ (not work) on
weekends, so Ryan ⁴ _____ __ (go) to
see friends in Puebla. Ryan ⁵ _____
(like) Mexico, but he ⁶ _____
(not speak) Spanish very well. He ⁷ _____
(have) a Spanish class on Sundays, and he
⁸ _____ (study) in the morning on
the bus. He ⁹ _____ (not watch) TV
because he ¹⁰ _____ (not understand)
the shows. He ¹¹ _____ (think)
Mexico is a fantastic country, and he
¹² _____ (not want) to go home.

c Complete the conversation with *do, does, don't,* or *doesn't.*

Mike	Hello, I'm Mike.
Sarah	Hi, I'm Sarah.
Mike	What ¹*do* _____ you do, Sarah?
Sarah	I'm a journalist.
Mike	² _____ you work for a newspaper?
Sarah	No, I ³ _____. I work for a magazine.
Mike	Where ⁴ _____ you work?
Sarah	I work in different places. At home, in the office, on the street…
Mike	⁵ _____ you like your job?
Sarah	Yes, I ⁶ _____. It's really interesting.
Mike	Where ⁷ _____ you live?
Sarah	I have a very small apartment near the park.
Mike	⁸ _____ you have brothers and sisters?
Sarah	Yes, I have one brother.
Mike	What ⁹ _____ he do?
Sarah	He works in a store.
Mike	¹⁰ _____ he have an apartment?
Sarah	No, he ¹¹ _____. He lives with our parents.

d Think of a friend or a member of your family and complete the sentences.

1 He / She lives in _____.
2 He / She likes _____.
3 He / She watches _____.
4 He / She drinks _____.
5 He / She has _____.

2 PRONUNCIATION third person *-es*

a ◖6.1 Listen and (circle) four more words with /ɪz/ and write them in the chart.

(closes) does eats finishes has goes likes listens lives loves reads relaxes speaks teaches wants watches works

/ɪz/	closes

b ◖6.1 Listen again and repeat the words.

3 VOCABULARY jobs and places of work

a Complete the puzzle. What's the mystery word?

b Complete the sentences.

1 A factory worker works in a f*actory*   .
2 A writer works at h_____.
3 A teacher works in a sc_____.
4 A waitress works in a r_____.
5 A policeman works on the st_____.
6 A nurse works in a h_____.
7 A salesperson works in a st_____.
8 A receptionist works in a hotel or an o_____.

4 PRONUNCIATION sentence rhythm

a 🔊6.2 Listen and complete the conversations.

1 A What *does*   *she*   do?
  B _____ _____ journalist.
  A _____ _____ like her job?
  B Yes, _____ _____.

2 A What _____ _____ do?
  B _____ _____ waiter.
  A Where _____ _____ work?
  B He _____ _____ _____ café.

b 🔊6.2 Listen again and repeat the sentences. Copy the rhythm.

5 WORDS AND PHRASES TO LEARN

Complete the conversations with a word or phrase from the list.

Because   Great to see you.
He's married to Lisa   How awful
I love your shoes   What does she do

1 A Who's that man with gray hair?
  B That's Hugo. *He's married to Lisa*.

2 A Maya, Karl, hi! _____.
  B Hello, Max. You too.

3 A _____ – they're beautiful!
  B Thank you – they're new.

4 A _____?
  B She's a nurse.

5 A Poor Yoko isn't very well. She's in the hospital.
  B Oh no! _____!

6 A Why do you get up at 5:30?
  B _____ I start work at 6:30.

🔄 Go online for more practice

6B Good morning, goodnight

Think in the morning.
Act in the afternoon. Eat in
the evening. Sleep at night.
*William Blake, British poet
and artist*

G adverbs of frequency **V** a typical day **P** /y/ and /yu/, sentence rhythm

1 VOCABULARY a typical day

a Complete the verb phrases.

1 g*et*_____ up   2 f_____ work

3 g_____ shopping   4 t_____ a shower

5 d_____ housework   6 m_____ dinner

7 w_____ TV   8 g_____ to bed

b Write the words in the chart.

~~to bed~~ ~~breakfast~~ a coffee dinner home
lunch a sandwich to school to the gym to work

have	go
breakfast	*to bed*

c Complete the text with the correct verbs.

do ~~finish~~ get up go (x4) have (x3) watch

I'm Mike, and I'm a factory worker. I work at
night and I sleep during the day. I ¹*finish*_____
work at eight o'clock in the morning, and then
I ²_____ home and I ³_____ to
bed. I ⁴_____ at about four o'clock in the
afternoon, and I ⁵_____ a big breakfast
— eggs, potatoes, sausages, and of course, a
lot of coffee! Then I ⁶_____ to the gym
after breakfast, then I ⁷_____ a shower
and I ⁸_____ TV. At seven o'clock in the
evening, I ⁹_____ dinner. Then I
¹⁰_____ to work again.

2 PRONUNCIATION /y/ and /yu/, sentence rhythm

a 🔊6.3 Listen and check (✓) the words that have the /y/ sound.

1 yellow	✓		6 easy	
2 factory	✗		7 boy	
3 young			8 your	
4 yogurt			9 gray	
5 ugly			10 yes	

b 🔊6.3 Listen again and repeat the words.

c 🔊6.4 Listen and check (✓) the words that have the /yu/ sound.

1 usually	✓		6 number	
2 umbrella	✗		7 beautiful	
3 study			8 future	
4 university			9 newspaper	
5 uniform			10 hurry	

d 🔊6.4 Listen again and repeat the words.

e 🔊6.5 Listen and complete the sentences.

1 I start work _at_ nine _in_ _the_ morning.
2 She _____ _____ coffee _____ _____ quarter _____ ten.
3 They _____ _____ sandwich _____ _____ café.
4 _____ finish work _____ six thirty.
5 _____ _____ housework _____ _____ weekend.
6 _____ watches TV _____ _____ evening.

f 🔊6.5 Listen again and repeat. <u>C</u>opy the <u>rhy</u>thm.

3 GRAMMAR adverbs of frequency

a Rewrite the sentences. Use the words in parentheses.

1 I get up early. (always)
   I always get up early.
2 Yasmin goes to school by bus. (usually)
   _____.
3 You do housework. (never)
   _____.
4 They have fish for dinner. (sometimes)
   _____.
5 Andy has lunch at home. (always)
   _____.
6 I watch TV in the morning. (never)
   _____.
7 We go shopping on weekends. (sometimes)
   _____.
8 They have coffee for breakfast. (usually)
   _____.

b Look at the chart and complete the sentences.

✓✓✓✓✓ = always
✓✓✓ = usually
✓ = sometimes
✗ = never

	Diego	Jen
go to the gym	✗	✓✓✓✓✓
read magazines	✓	✓✓✓
watch soccer on TV	✓✓✓✓✓	✓
get up early	✓✓✓	✗

1 Diego _never goes_ to the gym.
2 He _____ magazines.
3 He _____ soccer on TV.
4 He _____ early.
5 Jen _____ to the gym.
6 She _____ magazines.
7 She _____ soccer on TV.
8 She _____ early.

c Write about your typical evening. Use adverbs of frequency.

I always make dinner for my family. We usually eat at 7:00.

_____
_____
_____
_____
_____
_____

4 WORDS AND PHRASES TO LEARN

Complete the conversations with a word or phrase from the list.

~~Are you a morning person~~   every morning   feel tired
He gets up about 8:00   on the way to work
What time do you get up

1 A _Are you a morning person_?
   B Yes, I get up at 6:00 every day.

2 A _____?
   B I usually get up about 9:30. I don't get up early.

3 A What time does Harry get up?
   B _____.

4 A What do you do _____?
   B I usually read a magazine on the bus.

5 A What do you have for breakfast?
   B I have cereal and orange juice _____.

6 A Why do you go to bed at 8:30? It's very early.
   B Because I always _____ after work.

OXFORD
UNIVERSITY PRESS

198 Madison Avenue
New York, NY 10016 USA

Great Clarendon Street, Oxford, OX2 6DP, United Kingdom

Oxford University Press is a department of the University of Oxford. It furthers the University's objective of excellence in research, scholarship, and education by publishing worldwide. Oxford is a registered trade mark of Oxford University Press in the UK and in certain other countries

© Oxford University Press 2021

The moral rights of the author have been asserted

First published in 2021

2025 2024 2023

10 9 8 7

No unauthorized photocopying

All rights reserved. No part of this publication may be reproduced, stored in a retrieval system, or transmitted, in any form or by any means, without the prior permission in writing of Oxford University Press, or as expressly permitted by law, by licence or under terms agreed with the appropriate reprographics rights organization. Enquiries concerning reproduction outside the scope of the above should be sent to the ELT Rights Department, Oxford University Press, at the address above

You must not circulate this work in any other form and you must impose this same condition on any acquirer

Links to third party websites are provided by Oxford in good faith and for information only. Oxford disclaims any responsibility for the materials contained in any third party website referenced in this work

ISBN: 978 0 19 490603 6 MULTI-PACK A (PACK COMPONENT)

ISBN: 978 0 19 490602 9 MULTI-PACK A (PACK)

ISBN: 978 0 19 490586 2 ONLINE PRACTICE ACCESS CARD (PACK COMPONENT)

ISBN: 978 0 19 490607 4 ONLINE PRACTICE (PACK COMPONENT)

Printed in China

This book is printed on paper from certified and well-managed sources

STUDENT BOOK ACKNOWLEDGMENTS

Back cover photograph: Oxford University Press building/David Fisher

The authors would like to thank all the teachers and students around the world whose feedback has helped us to shape American English File.

The authors would also like to thank: all those at Oxford University Press (both in Oxford and around the world) and the design team who have contributed their skills and ideas to producing this course.

Finally very special thanks from Clive to Maria Angeles, Lucia, and Eric, and from Christina to Cristina, for all their support and encouragement. Christina would also like to thank her children Joaquin, Marco, and Krysia for their constant inspiration.

The publisher and authors are very grateful to the following who have provided personal stories and/or photographs: Hannah Donat and Dominic Latham-Koenig

The publisher and authors would also like to thank the following for their invaluable feedback on the materials: Magdalena Muszyńska, Brian Brennan, Krysia Mabbott, Dagmara Łata, Elif Barbaros, Zahra Bilides, Kenny McDonnell, Rosa María Iglesias Traviesas, Yolanda Calpe, Ana María Vallejo Guijarro, Patricia Ares

Sources: www.express.co.uk; www.dailymail.co.uk/femail/

We would also like to thank the following for permission to reproduce the following photographs: Cover: Hobbit/Shutterstock. 123RF pp 18 (one umbrella/Tatiana Popova), (four pencils/Liubov Shirokova), (two laptops/zentilia), 19 (E/Hemant Mehta); Alamy pp 9 (7/World Discovery), (man playing a buzuq/Rafael Ben-Ari), (man playing an accordian /Ilene Pearlman), (pan flute/YAY Media AS), (Drake/ZUMA Press, Inc.), (Korean drum/JIPEN), 10 (6/Shotshop GmbH), 12 (1/Michael Willis), (2/B Christopher), (3/Richard Sharrocks), (4/Martin Lee), 12 (British Tea/Denis Michaliov), 19 (A/Photoinke), (12/Paul Herbert), 20 (souvenir stand/Manor Photography), 22 (£10 GBP/Nick Fielding), (£10 Euros/Iakov Filimonov), ($10 US/Joe Sohm/Visions of America, LLC), 26 (Tizzy/Simon Stuart-Miller), (map/Digifoto Diamond), 27 (films/Everett Collection Inc), 34 (smartphone inset in A/Mike Abbott), (wristwatch repeated/musk), 45 (Alien Prometheus/AF archive), (Michael Fassbender/AF archive), 46 (Legionaries/Rolf Richardson), 48 (damaged car/Juha Jarvinen), (driving school car/B Christopher), 49 (6/Beaconstox), (8/Adrian Weston), 53 (Reading Terminal Market/Nikreates), 56 (fixing oven/Andriy Popov), 57 (Fat Face store/fc2/picturesbyrob), 59 (football/Sergio Azenha), (party/Mint Images Limited), (pizza party/LightField Studios Inc.), 60 (monster/Lake Champlain/Dale O'Dell), (Lake Champlain/ Robert Harding), 62 (AF archive), 64 (suit jacket/Oleksiy Maksymenko Photography), 65 (watching tv/Frank Sanchez), (New Orleans/Andreas von Einsiedel), 69 (boy shaving/Nick Moore), (cleaning shoes/ton koene), (cyclist/Frank Bienewald), 77 (woman on camel/age fotostock), 78 (10 Swatch/Richard Levine), 80 (museum/Alex Segre), 82 (10 Swatch/Richard Levine), 117 (3/blickwinkel), (5/JLImages), (7/AF archive), (10/View Pictures Ltd), (13/Prisma Bildagentur AG), 121 (Colours 6/Jeffrey Blackler), (Colours 8/Oleksiy Maksymenko Photography), (Adjectives 9/Jeffrey Blackler), 122 (sandwich/Barry Mason), (water/Gerhard Beneken/doc-stock), (Butter/Taylor Jorjorian), 123 (TV/Picture Partners), (drink tea/sebastiano volponi/MARKA), (bank/Image Source Plus), 124 (police officers/John Lord), (restaurant/Andrew Twort), (office/Hufton + Crow/View Pictures Ltd), (school/Art Directors & TRIP), (factory/Jim West), 126 (Travelling 12/Juice Images), (Free Time 2/Kevin Britland), (Free Time 11/Jeff Morgan 01), (Travelling 6/Terese Loeb Kreuzer), (Travelling 7/Peter Titmuss), (Travelling 8/Kumar Sriskandan), (Travelling 9/Jeff Greenberg), 128 (9/Keenretail); Courtesy of David Clarke p 56 (wearing a suit); Hannah Donat p38 (Hannah and Kit); Getty Images pp 8 (2/Onoky - Fabrice Lerouge), (Caetano Veloso/Damian Dopacio/AFP), (Lila Downs/Omar Vega/LatinContent Editorial), 9 (1/Joey Foley/Getty Images Entertainment), (2/Jupiterimages/The Image Bank), (4/Egyptian), (10/Jon Furniss/WireImage), (12/Gustavo Caballero/Getty Images Entertainment), 13 (1/Jerod Harris/Getty Images Entertainment), (4/Jim Spellman/WireImage), (Shawn Mendes/Mark Sagliocco), 16 (pen/Donald Erickson/Collection E+), 17 (Mark/NicolasMcComber/E+), 20 (NY Yankees cap/Robtek), (t-shirt logo/FarbaKolerova), 28 (wallet/Creative Crop), 29 (Jeremy Fisher and family/Philip and Karen SmithCollection/Photographer's Choice RF), (Claire and her sisters/Westend61), 30 (Sakura/Tadamasa Taniguchi), (coffee in office/Gregor Schuster), 35 (tired/Christopher Hope-Fitch), (hungry/John Lund/Marc Romanelli/Blend Images), (hot/Cultura/Chris Whitehead), (thirsty/Peter Cade/Iconica), 36 (1/Chris Condon/US PGA Tour), (3/Frederic Lucano/The Image Bank), 42 (Polly and Andrew/Antenna), 46 (JK Rowling/Dave J Hogan/Getty Images Europe), 49 (2/Bloomberg via Getty Images), (3/Digital Vision/Riou), (4/lbusca), (5/Oliver Strewe/Lonely Planet Images), (9/Jung Yeon-Je/AFP), 52 (couple on plane/fStop Images/Halfdark), (artist/Caiaimage/Rafal Rodzoch), 57 (1/Gary Alvis), (Sandra/Juanmonino), 60 (Inn Hotel/Education Images), (Hotel Room/Jumping Rocks), 64 (shoes/Stuart Burr), 65 (balcony/Ferad Zyulkyarov/Moment), (Gumbo/LauriPatterson), 66 (plane/Bloomberg), (restaurant/ EmirMemedovski), 78 (2/Visual China Group), (3/Giuseppe Cacace/AFP), (4/Alex Davies/FilmMagic), (5/Michael Melford/National Geographic Magazines), (6/Victor Virgile/Gamma-Rapho), (7/Bloomberg), (9/Jose Perez Gegundez/Gamma-Rapho), 80 (restaurant/Andrew Holt Collection/Photographer's), 82 (reused from p78), 86 (Breakfast/ Siraphol Siricharattakul / EyeEm), 117 (2/Luis Castaneda Inc.), (6/Izzet Keribar), (Brazil/Peetatham Kongkapech), (Canada/Matteo Colombo), (Chile/Ebba Gregorsson Lundius), (China/Dong Wenjie), (England/Fabio Flgel/EyeEm0), (Japan/DoctorEgg), (Peru/Kelly Cheng Travel Photography), (Saudi Arabia/Katharina Kuntz / EyeEm), (Turkey/Christy Turner Photography / 500px), (Grand Canyon/Dean Fikar), (Vietnam/efired), 120 (People 1/Stefka Pavlova/Moment Open), (People 2/Gen Umekita), (grandparents/aldomurillo), 121 (Colours 9/Nikada/E+), (Adjectives 2/Michael Melford/Photographer's Choice), (Adjectives 5/Car Culture), (Adjectives 6/Ken Ishii/Getty Images AsiaPac), (fast car/ Hirkophoto), (slow car/Johner Images - Wikstrom, Jeppe), 123 (radio/Frontdoor Images/Stone), (dog/Rafael Elias), (cats/Cultura/Zak Kendal), (broken down car/Rhienna Cutler/E+), 124 (journalist/Max Mumby/Indigo), (shop assistant/Bloomberg), (receptionist/Frederic Lucano/The Image Bank), (factory worker/Monty Rakusen/Cultura), (cab driver/Jupiterimages/Photolibrary), (department store/Bloomberg), (desk at home /Westend61), (police officers/Kali 9), 126 (Free Time 1/Blend Images/Jose Luis Pelaez Inc), (Free Time 4/Robert Daly/Ojo Images), (Free Time 5/Morsa Images), (Free Time 8/Stock4B), (Travelling 2/Andersen Ross/Blend Images), (Travelling 11/Emma Innocenti/Taxi), (sunglasses/Hero Images), 128 (14/Philippe Lissac/Corbis Documentary), (17/vgajic/E+), (movies/Chris Hondros); Phil Hill @ United National Photographers p 56 (David Clarke working in hotel); iStockphoto p 42 (man washing up/Graham Oliver); Christina Latham-Koenig pp 37; Dominic Latham-Koenig p 66 (Dominic and family), 66 (Dominic's house), 67; Reproduced by permission of Oxford University Press from Oxford Essential Dictionary © Oxford University Press 2012 pp 16 (dictionary); Reproduced by permission of Oxford University Press p 66 cover of *SPLAT!* (2017) By Jon Burgerman and cover of *Mr Bunny's Chocolate Factory* (2017) by Elys Dolan; OUP pp 18 (one pencil), 20 (Manhattan Map/Catherine Johnson), (keychain/Catherine Johnson), (Mug/Catherine Johnson), (Teddy Bear/Catherine Johnson), 22 (50 cents), 25 (Bday card/Catherine Johnson), 40 (bread), (orange juice), 59 (sandwich), 117 (9), 119 (debit card/Catherine Johnson), (passport/Catherine Johnson), (Phone Charger/ Catherine Johnson), 120 (Family 1 & 2), (Family 7-8/Image Source/Getty Images), 121 (Adjectives 15), (Adjectives 16), 129 (suit); OUP\Alamy pp 16 (whiteboard/RTimages), (door/Dmytro Grankin), 22 (50 pence/Images), 35 (cold/XiXinXing), 49 (1/Perry van Munster), (7/Esa Hiltula), 52 (camping/Stockbroker), 57 (3/Dudley Wood), 59 (coffee/Piotr Skubisz), 64 (suit trousers/Creative Control), 84 (couple/Juice Images), (opening times/Jack Carey), 86 (family), 116 (Sean Gladwell), 117 (4/Jan Tadeusz), (8/Sean Pavone), 120 (People 6/Image Source), (Family 3-6/D. Hurst), (Family 11-12/Ojo Images Ltd), 121 (Colours 3/Marek Kosmal), (Colours 7/Nalinratana Phiyanalinmat), (Colours 10/Artem Merzlenko), (Adjectives 10/Picturebank), 122 (yoghurt/FoodFood), (milk/Valentyn Volkov), (orange juice/imageBroker), (man drinking/Mint Images), 123 (flat/UpperCut Images), (breakfast/UpperCut Images), (newspaper/Juice Images), (speak English/Andres Rodriguez), (want coffee/Image Source Plus), (polystyrene cup/Judith Collins), (classes/Cathy Topping), 124 (nurse/OJO Images Ltd), (hospital/Zoonar GmbH), 126 (Travelling 10/Hybrid Images/Image Source Salsa); OUP\Corbis pp 17 (Bianca), 122 (vegetables), 123 (fast food); OUP\DAJ p122 (tea); OUP\Photodisc p 22 (25 cents); OUP\Photolibrary pp 8 (1), 22 (25 cents), 59 (coke), 87, 122 (eggs), 124 (doctor); OUP\Shutterstock pp 18 (picture frame/pixelheadphoto digitalskillet), 27 (houses/Ewelina Wachala), 41 (Japanese food/bonshan), 119 (newspaper), 122 (salad/Kuttelvaserova Stuchelova); REX/Shutterstock pp 19 (D/Pablo Martinez Monsivais/AP), 45 (Charlize Theron /Scott Free Prod/20th Century Fox/Kobal), (Sigourney Weaver/Dennis Cameron), (Alien (original)/20th Century Fox/Kobal), (AlienCovenant/Rob Latour), 46 (The Lord of the Rings/New Line/Kobal), (Star Wars/Lucasfilm/Fox/Kobal), 121 (Adjectives 7/Image Broker), (Adjectives 8/John O'Reilly), 128 (18 still from'House' on TV screen/Fox-TV/Kobal); Shutterstock pp 8 (3/bezikus), (back view couple/Kamenetskiy Konstantin), (wall/rangizzz), (pavement/donatas1205), (poster graphic/ balabolka), 9 (6/Vereshchagin Dmitry), (8/Scharfsinn), (9/Lev Kropotov), 10 (1/Jordan Tan), (2/chrisdorney), (3/Marija Stojkovic), (4/Claudio Divizia), (5/Stephen Coburn), (7/Sergio Monti Photography), (8/Jack Jelly), 13 (2/Waldemar Dabrowski), (3/Dawid Lech), (Samsung phone/Nemanja Zotovic), 16 (chair/Just2shutter), 17 (Jacek/LightField Studios), 18 (book/Amero), (semi-closed laptop/Peter Kotoff), (phone/RikoBest), (smiling woman/Kim Diaz), (open laptop/Nata-Lia), (three umbrellas/Anton-Burakov), 19 (B/Atstock Productions), (C/stockfour), (1/natushm), (2/Brilliance stock), (3/Nitikorn Poonsiri), (4/David Baumgartner), (5/alexialex), (6/kozirsky), (7/Jakraphong Photography), (8/Claudio Divizia), (9/mrkornflakes), (10/akiyoko), (11/aPhoenixPhotographer), 20 (sunglasses/exopixel), (postcard/Tupungato), (Sunglasses/Shutterstock), (t-shirt/Africa Studio), 24 (boy/list), (girl/list), (man/list), (woman/list), 26 (car logos/Rose Carson), (Hyundai logo/IgorGolovniov), (Geely logo/ Piotr Swat), (Seat logo/Mdogan), (blue smart car/Grzegorz Czapski), 27 (cities/segawa7), (food/Onchira Wongsiri), (restaurants/SPhoto), (books/Billion Photos), (dogs/InBetweentheBlinks), (photos/bepsy), 28 (umbrella/burnel1), (credit card/yablueko), (key/Winai Tepsuttinun), (cap/Etaphop photo), (teddy/Num LPPhoto), 30 (sandwich/gowithstock), (eggs/Africa Studio), (tea/M. Unal Ozmen), (cheese/Nattika), (orange juice/Africa Studio), (Marta/Kudryashova Alla), (Paulo/LightField Studios), (Rob/Azovtsev Maksym), (coffee cup/3DMAVR), (tea mug/Evlakhov Valeriy), 34 (clock graphic 1-6/Lightkite), 36 (2/wavebreakmedia), 37 (Antonio/David Tadevosian), (Charlotte/Africa Studio), (nurse/Monkey Business Images), (hospital background/Joachim Heng), 38 (avocado/NatashaPhoto), (bath/stocksolutions), 40 (water/Gyvafoto), (sugar/Sea Wave), (milk/Jon Le-Bon), (cheese), 42 (woman watching tv/antoniodiaz), (couple/mentatdgt), 46 (keyboard/Guguart), (Fifth Avenue/Tono Balaguer), 49 (speed limit sign/Charles Lewis), 50 (1/Mima Antic), (2/Erin Cadigan), (3/CKP1001), (Isabella/Twin Sails), (William/VGstockstudio), (Angie/Taras Atamaniv), (Daniel/Dean Drobot), (Adriana/De Repente), (Luke/Dean Drobot), 52 (cycling/Ljupco Smokovski), (cooking/Robert Kneschke), (man with suitcase/leolintang), (jogging/Dean Drobot), (swimming/Suzanne Tucker), 57 (2/Karkas), (4/Chiyacat), (5/Mariyana M), (Rue 21/Jonathan Weiss), (young woman/Aaron Amat), 59 (salad/Christian Jung), (party/Monkey Business Images), (concert/melis), 60 (Vermont Map/AridOcean), 61 (view through the window/Alinute Silzeviciute), 63 (digital clock 7 am and 10am/creatOR76), (digital clock 4 pm and 6.30pm/Macrovector), (wristwatch/MarySan), (Jason's wife/Spectral-Design), 64 (dress/Karkas), (jacket/mates), (shirt/OZaiachin), (skirt/Karkas), (trousers/Elnur), (hat/Slavko Sereda), 65 (Jenna/Wayhome studio), (couple/ Wayhome studio), (tapas/Andreas Saldavs), (watching tv female legs only/MarinaP), (Football/Jamie Lamor Thompson), 66 (Lego helicopter/cjmacer), (mountain landscape on booking screen/Dave Allen Photography), (suitcases/Laborant), 68 (hallway background/Africa Studio), 69 (sky dive/Sky Antonio), (wedding/IVASHstudio), 75 (dice/Gearstd), 77 (Petra/liseykina), 78 (1/Ratthaphong Ekariyasap), (8/Brent Hofacker), (Mt. Fuji/ Jagapong Saenphab), (Machu Piccu/ Ivan_off), (Hyundai car/ Dmitry Eagle Orlov), (Pepsi & Coke can/Mejini Neskah), 79 (clocks/Lightkite), 81 (charger/Passakorn sakulphan), (purse/A N D A), (iPad/nixki), (Canadian passports/dennizn), 82 (1/Ratthaphong Ekariyasap), (8), (10 Rolex/list), 83 (clocks/Lightkite), 85 (surprised people/Dima Sidelnikov), 117 (1/Mark Schwettmann), (11/vvoe), (12/Sean Pavone), (14/Luciano Mortula), (15/Critterbiz), (Argentina/Carolina Bello), (Korea/ Teerachat paibung), (Mexico/ Patryk Kosmider), 119 (Hungarian passport/Abihatsira Issac), (credit card/Popular Business), 120 (People 3/Nadino), (People 4/magedb.com), (People 5/Andresr), (Family 9-10/wavebreakmedia), 121 (Colours 1/Elnur), (Colours 2/Pabkov), (Colours 4/Yganko), (Colours 5/Evgen3dstudio), (Adjectives 1/pics721), (Adjectives 3/jannoon028), (Adjectives 4/SmileStudio), (Adjectives 11/Natasha Kramskaya), (Adjectives 12/Yuralaits Albert), (Adjectives 13/panpote), (Adjectives 14/psirob), 122 (fish/HLPhoto), (meat/Valentyn Volkov), (pasta/chrisbrignell), (rice/leungchopan), (potatoes/isak55), (fruit/Africa Studio), (bread/Tim UR), (butter/Photographee.eu), (cheese/Tim UR), (sugar/GayvoronskayaYana), (cereal/Oliver Hoffmann), (chocolate/Yeko Photo Studio), (coffee/Artem and Olga Sapegin), (wine/lenetstan), (beer/Tarasyuk Igor), (woman eating /159877448), 123 (woman w/ coffee/Kinga), 124 (teacher/wavebreakmedia), (waiters/Dmitry Kalinovsky), (street with police/Dutourdumonde Photography), 126 (Free Time 3/Tono Balaguer), (Free Time 6/Andresr), (Free Time 7/Galyna Andrushko), (Satyrenko), (Free Time 10/Lucky Business), (Free Time 12/Teri Virbickis), (Travelling 4/Robert Kneschke), (Travelling 5/Cookie Studio), (gym/nd3000), (tennis/George Rudy), (buying souvenirs/Denis Koryakin), 128 (1/ESB Professional), (2/Kiselev Andrey Valerevich), (3/merzzie), (4/Cultura Motion), (5/I AM NIKOM), (7/Akimov Igor), (8/Syda Productions), (10/David Tadevosian), (11/Andrii Kobryn), (12/nd3000), (13/Minerva Studio), (15/baranq), (16/Halfpoint), (18 people watching TV/wavebreakmedia), (yoga/David Tadevosian), 129 (cap/Ukki Studio), (hat/rawisoot), (coat/elenovsky), (dress/Vlad Teodor), (jacket/Peter Versnel), (jeans/gresei), (shirt/Elnur), (green shoes/Magdalena Wielobob), (skirt/Karkas), (socks/ConstantinosZ), (sweater/elenovsky), (T-shirt/Iasha), (trainers/BornRichjapan), (grey trousers/demidoff), (shorts/windu).

Pronunciation chart artwork by: Ellis Nadler

Illustrations by: Amber Day/Illustration Ltd. pp 12, 13, 36; Jo Bird/Jelly London: p44 (illustrated background), 70-71 (map), 81, 85; Stephen Collins pp 125, 130; Clementine Hope/NB.Illustration Ltd. pp 14 (illustrated background), 54, 55, 61 (illustrated backgrounds), 80 & 84 (bedrooms); Laura Perez/Anna Goodson Illustration Agency pp 32-33, 64; Claire Rollet p 21 (illustrated background), 79; Ben Swift/NB.Illustration Ltd. p26 (illustrated background); John Haslam pp 80 & 84 ('the same or different'), 92, 93, 94, 96, 97, 98, 99, 100, 101, 102, 104, 106, 109, 110, 115, 118, 126

Commissioned photography by: Gareth Boden pp 24, 25 (family); 44, 48-49 (Anna and instructor), 68 (people), 72, 73 (having coffee); MM Studios pp 6, 7, 14 (people), 20 (stallholder), 21 (people), 25 (Jane, Marina and card), 26 (people), 30 (breakfasts for Marta, Paulo and Sakura), 44 (people) 61 (ball and remote control), 66 (book covers), 81, 86 (breakfast), 119 (Hungarian ID card), 123 (study), 126 (Travelling 1), 126 (Travelling 3), 128: (eating out 6); Oxford University Press video stills pp 11, 15, 20 (stall holder), 17 (vox pops), 22 (menu), 23, 27 (Beaulieu), 29 (vox pops), 34 (Rob and Alan), 35 (Jenny and Amy), 39, 41 (vox pops), 47, 51, 53 (vox pops), 58, 59 (meeting a friend), 63 (hotel), 65 (vox pops), 71, 73 (in car, at concert, Royal Albert Hall), 77 (vox pops).

Although every effort has been made to trace and contact copyright holders before publication, this has not been possible in some cases. We apologize for any apparent infringement of copyright and if notified, the publisher will be pleased to rectify any errors or omissions at the earliest opportunity.

WORKBOOK ACKNOWLEDGMENTS

The publisher would like to thank the following for their permission to reproduce photographs: Cover: Hobbit/Shutterstock. **Alamy** pp.6 (American woman/Golden Pixels LLC), 8 (NBA/Grzegorz Knec, JFK/Patti McConville, ET/AF archive), 14 (newspaper/Clynt Garnham Publishing), 15 (ID card/Dinodia Photos), 18 (5p/Studioshots, £10/Tades Yee), 23 (Ben Molyneux Spanish Collection), 24 (Butter/Taylor Jorjorian), 26 (Lucas/Julio Bulnes), 31 (3/Hero Images Inc.), (7/Robert Convery) (policewoman/Ira Berger), 40 (3/Kumar Sriskandan), 44 (2/iPhone, 3/Neil Guegan), (hailing cab/Eric Carr), 45 (6/Takatoshi Kurikawa, 9/Cultura Creative (RF)), 49 (Panther Media GmbH); **Getty Images** pp.6 (vase/Heritage Images), (Machu Picchu/Lívia Auler), (middle eastern man/michaeljung), 9 (hotel reception/valentinrussanov/E+), 24 (yogurt/Axel Bueckert/EyeEm), 26 (café), 30 (smiling woman/electravk), (smiling man/funky-data), 32 (factory worker/kali9), 44 (dialing phone/Hero Images); **Oxford University Press** pp.6 (Brazil, England), 8 (whiteboard, laptop, pen, door, chair, window, dictionary), 10 (all), 14 (wallet, watch, umbrella, bag, glasses, photo frame, credit card, ID card, tablet), (newspaper/Alamy/OUP), 15 (dictionary, keys, frame, pens, door, table, coats), 16 (Teddy Bear/Catherine Johnson), (Manhattan Map/Catherine Johnson), 24 (all crossword food), 29 (1, 2, 3, 5), 38 (both), 40 (1, 2, 4, 5), 44 (4, 5), 45 (7, 10, 11, 12), 46 (man working, students outside); **Rex Shutterstock** pp. 6 (Canada soccer fan/Yves Logghe/AP/REX), 25 (man holding books/Jaybranding Studio), 30 (smiling man/AJR_photo), 36 (Ghost 1990/Paramount/Kobal), (My Fair Lady 1964/Warner Bros/Kobal), (Titanic 1997/Moviestore), 37 (Skyfall 2012/Danjaq/EON Productions/Kobal), (Dumb and Dumber 1995/Moviestore), (Twelve Years A Slave 2013/Regency Enterprises/Kobal), (Kung Fu Panda 2 2011/Dreamworks Animation/Kobal), (Django Unchained 2012/Columbia/The Weinstein Company/Kobal), (Carrie 2013/AF archive, Star Trek Beyond 2016/Paramount Pictures/Bad Robot/Kobal); **Shutterstock** pp.6 (Mexico/Rui Vale Sousa), (Japan/Vincent St. Thomas), (China/Zhao Jian Kang), (Spain/Kavalenkau), (Italian woman/Izabela Magier), (Manuel Neuer/Dmytro Larin), (sugar skull/BestStockFoto), (Japanese woman/takayuki), (Javier Bardem/Andrea Raffin), (bibimbap/Dia pic), 8 (ID badge/Paul Paladin, SOS/Choi Jae Young, table/Kaspars Grinvalds, rucksack/Rusly95, coat/photo25th, paper/Peter Kotoff), 12 (women/Antonio Guillem, woman on phone/Antonio Guillem, man on phone/fizkes), 14 (USA passport/charles taylor), (camera/Billion Photos), (notebook/Vitaly Korovin), (phone/Nemanja Zotovic), (pencil/Sarawut Aiemsinsuk), (key/Ilya Akinshin), 16 (cap/Pixfiction), (keyring/Alicja Neumiler), (mug/windu), (t-shirt/Surrphoto), (sunglasses/exopixel), (postcard/Tupungato), 18 (one US cent/NY-P), ($100 note/Chones), (20 euro cent/jooh), (£50 note/Chones), 24 (top man/ESB Professional), (man in hat/mimagephotography), (woman with glasses/WAYHOME studio), (bottom woman/WAYHOME studio), 25 (Alessandra/El Nariz), (children/Evgeny Atamanenko), 29 (4/mimagephotography), 30 (Luis/mimagephotography), 31 (1/michaeljung, 2/Monkey Business Images), (4/Kzenon), (5/ESB Professional), (6/Africa Studio), (7/Africa Studio), (8/GaudiLab, 9/StockLite), 33 (Diego/wavebreakmedia), (Jen/Monkey Business Images), 39 (antpkr), 40 (no music/astudio), 45 (8/Dmytro Zinkevych), (airport terminal/SIHASAKPRACHUM), 46 (gallery/Popova Valeriya), (man in suit/sanneberg), (college students in park studying/Dean Drobot), 50 (11/Selin Aydogan), (3/medvedsky.kz), (toilet/Milkovasa), 52 (Jacob Lund), 59 (Kirayonak Yuliya), 60 (franz12), 61 (AboutLife), 62 (Ruslan Guzov), 63 (Monkey Business Images).

Pronunciation chart artwork: by Ellis Nadler

Illustrations by: Mark Duffin pp.24 (meals), 28, 50 (1, 2, 4, 5, 6, 7, 8, 9, 10, 12); Atushi Hara/Dutch Uncle pp.32; Adam Larkum/Illustration Ltd. p.47, 58; Sean Longcroft pp.20 (ex 2), 27, 41, 42, 53, 56; Roger Penwill pp.4, 5, 16, 17, 20 (ex 1), 22, 34, 51, 54.